The Language of Excellence

This book has the capacity to create a conversation
that can lead you and your team to greatness.

Visit *www.i65north.com*

Cover design by Tom Trebing

ISBN: 978-0-9856673-4-4
Library of Congress Control Number: 2013922725

Other titles by M. Thomas (Tom) Collins

The Claret Murders: A Mark Rollins Adventure

Mark Rollins and the Puppeteer

Mark Rollins and the Rainmaker

Mark Rollins' New Career & the Women's Health Club

*Marion Collins Remembers Old
Sayings and Lessons for Life*

My Journey: Alice Elsie Welch Collins

The Language of Excellence

By

TOM COLLINS

This book is a testament to the power of the flip chart and the whiteboard. Visit any innovative organization and you will find them throughout. *The Wall Street Journal* called the whiteboard "high tech's secret weapon."

CONTENTS

Section II
Change: The Path to Excellence

Section III
Management: Guidelines for Excellence

Section IV
Opportunities: Strategies for Excellence

Section V
People: The Foundation for Excellence

Section VI
Action: The Final Ingredient for Excellence

Section VII
Executive Overview

FOREWORD

A Romanian accountant walks into the office and asks . . .

In the mid-1990s, I was faced with the question: How do you teach a Romanian financial employee about business management and strategy? In 1996, I was an expatriate finance professional working for Colgate-Palmolive and had taken on the management of the finance team for Colgate Romania. While I had traveled in Eastern Europe for several years, this was my first permanent assignment, and I looked forward to teaching the young team about capitalism. Young Eastern European professionals simply did not have the benefit of context when it came to management concepts.

I thought about assigning them a diet of management books but then remembered that my father had put together an "everyman's" template of readily teachable material that at the time was known as the *ABCs of Insearch*. I still have one of the original copies he gave me more than thirty years ago. While I had referenced the material from time to time in the early stages of my career, for the first time I looked at the entire body of work and understood its purpose. Simply put, he had taken the most fundamental elements of management theory and practice from dozens of experts and distilled the content into simple and readily teachable images and phrases for the purpose of aligning an entire organization from top to bottom. It was genius.

I have carried this material around with me from Eastern Europe to the early days of the Internet boom when I joined a start-up in NYC named DoubleClick, eventually serving as both Chief Financial Officer and Chief Technology Officer of that NASDAQ-traded public company. I then joined my father at Juris, Inc., taking over the lead of the organization as Dad battled cancer. As he recovered, I had the pleasure of working and learning from him for a few years until we sold the company to LexisNexis. More recently, I was at another NASDAQ company, Bazaarvoice—initially serving as its Chief Financial Officer and then as Chief Executive Officer of the Internet social commerce company. No matter where I have worked—I have worked in dozens of countries around the world—and no matter the business context, I continue to discover and marvel at the incredible utility of what is now titled *The Language of Excellence*.

I owe an incredible debt of gratitude to my father for the gift of this content. It has guided me and will continue to guide me as I evolve as a business leader and entrepreneur. I have shared the material on many occasions and the concepts are embedded, perhaps unknowingly, into any number of companies spread through the people I have had the privilege to work with throughout my career. My father has had more influence than he even knows in this regard, and it is truly wonderful to see him update the material and translate it to the age of the whiteboard.

After many years in business, I still find *The Language of Excellence* to be the most useful and powerful management-teaching tool I've come across. I hope you, the reader, will too.

Dad, thank you for this incredible legacy.

Stephen R. Collins

PREFACE

I have been called one of the pioneers of the information technology service industry. It is more accurate to say I have lived several business lives in the course of my career. I started my journey as a CPA with Price Waterhouse & Co., now PricewaterhouseCoopers. Since then I participated in the boom-and-bust of the franchise movement, the conglomerate age, and a dozen iterations of the technology industry—from service bureaus, to remote processing computer utilities, to online services, to turnkey minicomputers, and then the democratizational impact of the personal computer.

I have been hired, fired, gone public, gone private, and been both acquirer and acquired. By the mid-1980s, I thought I was retiring early to enjoy the good life. An associate, however, asked me to help narrow their business focus by selling off some of their smaller product lines. One of those was a small turnkey minicomputer group specializing in law firm business systems. Rather than selling it, I bought it. Just about that time, IBM introduced the PC, Novell figured out how to connect them into a network, and WordPerfect introduced word processing software for the PC. While the entrenched market leaders at the time were laughing off the PC as a toy, my new company, Juris, Inc., was taking over market leadership by capitalizing on the convergence of those three events.

Juris, Inc. was quite different from all my other business ventures. It came late in my career at a time when I did not have to worry about meeting the next payroll. There were no public shareholders, investment houses, or outside directors who had to be appeased. And I was smarter. I had learned that teaching people was more effective than directing them. In addition, I had taken the time in the year preceding the purchase, to document my core beliefs about business—the early version of what I now call *The Language of Excellence.*

Juris, Inc. is gone—purchased by LexisNexis in 2007. The product line and Juris name continue under the LexisNexis umbrella. While some former Juris team members remain with LexisNexis, most have moved on. A few, like me, are retired. I continue to get e-mails and calls from many people thanking me for the Juris experience—something best described as a conversation in the pursuit of excellence. In fact, this book is for them, in response to their requests that I write it.

Thanks, team, for a great conversation.

INTRODUCTION

This book is simple. It has the capacity to create a conversation that can lead you and your team to greatness. It is a conversation that will move the know-how to achieve excellence from the back of the brain to the front. It will make doing and saying the right things—making the right decisions and avoiding the wrong ones—a habit.

The concepts inside this book apply to life as well as business. This book is one of the best gifts one could give to a young professional. It can be invaluable to the entrepreneur starting a new business or to a seasoned executive frustrated by the difficulty of steering an unresponsive corporate ship.

I wrote this book as a teaching aid. I discovered by accident that when all members of an organization understand the implications of important management and leadership concepts, magic happens within that enterprise. It is as if someone pulls back the curtain and turns up the lights. Suspicions disappear, replaced by unity. To learn about the behavior of *change*, to gain an understanding of the *rule of the fewest*, to be able to put a name to observed phenomena such as the *life cycle* and *suboptimization* tears down the iron curtain between "management" and "employees." A team arises—a competent team, one that shares a core set of beliefs and a common sense of direction—eager to help write their own playbook.

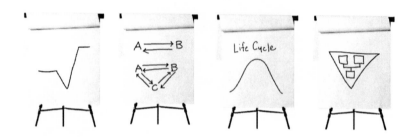

I created the early version of this work in 1986 when I started Juris, Inc. with only about a dozen employees. We met at noon each day in our new conference room. While the rest of the team ate lunch, I manned the flip chart or the whiteboard. During that hour, we would discuss some of the graphic images representing important business concepts—images like the following model for excellence:

The conversation was not confined to the conference room. That is because the names of images are trigger words. A reference to the *change curve*, for example, triggers the visual image in the mind's eye and the mind recalls the behavior of change and its implications.

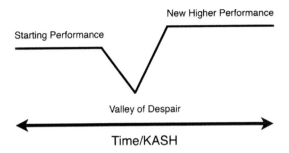

Our everyday conversation began to include phrases like "Count the Teeth," "Mack Truck problem," "Authority Triangle," and "Management Candy."

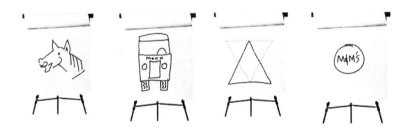

The graphic images and their trigger words became a self-sustaining conversation that continually refreshed and reinforced sound management concepts. It was a conversation transcending geographic and organizational lines to bind us together as a unified team.

Because the graphic images and trigger words were part of Juris, Inc. from the beginning, its spread to new team members (including those in our dealers' organizations) was organic. Being part of Juris meant you were part of "the conversation." You could not be a member of Juris and avoid being in the conversation.

The task of starting that conversation in an established company, especially a larger one, requires a more deliberate approach, but it is a proven one. You start by teaching the teachers. It is a natural progression following the organization chart. The CEO or COO teaches the division heads, who teach the department heads, who teach the unit leaders, who teach members of the unit. Once the conversation has started, organic growth will take over. In a large organization, dedicated trainers can eventually take on the task of bringing new team members up-to-date so they can join the conversation.

As valuable as I believe this book will be to you, it is an unfinished work. There is nothing that says you cannot add your own graphics and your own trigger words. Why shouldn't there be one for "eat our own cooking" to set the standard that, as an organization, you would never inflict something new on your customers without having first experienced it yourself? This book is a big head start, but there is still plenty of room to make it your own. As important as all the concepts in this book are to me, there are probably others particularly important to your organization.

I want to clarify that I claim no origination credit for the concepts I have included. They are a compilation of ideas collected, distilled, reshaped, blogged, and even tweeted during fifty years of on-the-job training and a lifetime of reading and listening to the great minds of business—men like Peter Drucker, W. Edwards Deming, and Tom Peters. The use of graphics and trigger words that bring those visual images to mind was inspired by usability improvements contributed by icons in graphical user interfaces (GUIs), by the power of Tom Peters's model of excellence, and by the effectiveness of

Model-Netics, the graphic image-laden management training courses of American General during my brief tenure with the company.

Nor do I believe I am going to teach you much that you do not already know. Some of the concepts in this book are intuitive—or just plain old common sense. Some you may have learned at your father's knee or on your mother's lap. Others you probably gleaned from books or learned from teachers, mentors, or firsthand experience. Some you will have picked up from conferences or lectures. Perhaps you will find a few new ideas herein, but that is not my main objective.

My purpose is to give you and your team the capacity for a conversation that will lead to excellence. It is a system of using graphics and trigger words to communicate and reinforce an organization's core beliefs. It is a conversation that will empower members of your team with the confidence to take the right action *while they are on the front line*—when they are confronted with a decision to make, a problem to solve, or an opportunity to pursue. I am going to move the know-how for achieving excellence from the back of the brain to the front. I am going to help you make doing and saying the right things—making the right decisions and avoiding the wrong ones—a habit.

I have given you a starter set for that conversation. You can make it your own.

Section I

I-65 North:

The Pursuit of Excellence

I-65 North

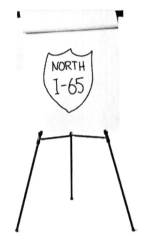

"I-65 North" is a metaphor about business.

Business is a journey; one that involves constant change and where success is determined through the eyes of those who judge us. The role of a leader is to get people moving in the same direction toward a common destination with a clear understanding of the rules of the road for getting there. I-65 North conveys the idea of a journey with everyone traveling in the same direction—north. North is analogous to the idea of upward progress (the pursuit of excellence).

While the destination of the business journey is set and communicated by an organization's leader, individuals are not robots. If you are on the team, it is because the organization believes in you as an achiever, but many things shape how each member of the team performs in pursuit of the destination. There is not one performance style that has a monopoly on success. The analogy of the interstate conveys this flexibility. Individuals determine their own rate of speed on the journey north, provided they do not go so slow as to impede others or so fast as to recklessly endanger others. As an individual within the organization, however, you cannot go south, east, or west. You as an individual are in control. It is your vehicle, but the leader sets the direction and destination.

Business is a journey. The role of the leader is to get everyone traveling in the same direction.

Two Certainties

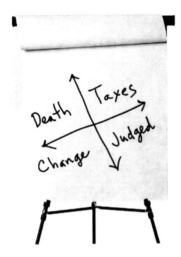

Change is constant and others will always judge us.

The term "death and taxes" in the flip chart image is often quoted as the two certainties in life. The graphic pairs those commonsense terms with the words "change" and "judged" because *change* and *judged* are better descriptions of the two certainties as faced by businesses.

Benjamin Franklin voiced simple truths. He understood the two certainties and he stated them in simple terms of his day—*death* and *taxes*. *Death* represents the ultimate human change, and a *tax* is the assessment or judgment of government. For deliberate long-term success, an enterprise must have an understanding and acceptance of the two certainties—(1) we either purposely change to improve, or natural forces erode and change us for the worse, and (2) what we are is determined through the judgment of others.

I vividly remember the visuals and dialogue of a TV commercial in which a young man, a skinhead with tattooed arm sleeves and multiple piercings, is talking to the camera while smoking. Let's call him Charley. He declares, "I just want to be judged for who I am!"

Well, Charley, that is exactly what is happening. You are being judged for who you are. You are a skinhead! You have lots of tattoos and piercings. In addition, while an increasing number of people find smoking to be offensive, you are very public about doing so. The thing Charley is missing is that he does not get to tell us who he is. We decide that. Not just by how he looks, but also by how he conducts himself. Based on what we know about Charley right now, he has a shot at being a success if he is joining a rock band, but if he is looking for a career in banking or finance, then as my friends in Brooklyn would say, "Fuhgeddaboudit." There is nothing optional about the two certainties. That is why we call them *certainties*!

For long-term purposeful success, you must learn to deal with and manage change, and you must accept that you and your accomplishments are what others perceive them to be.

We change to improve, or natural forces will change us for the worse; and we are defined by how others see us.

MODEL FOR EXCELLENCE

Excellence is the only sound strategy.

In the above model, the top of the pyramid represents excellence. The foundation is people. Excellence can only be achieved through people who truly care about their customers, the left side of the pyramid. The eye signifies that you do not determine when or if you achieve excellence. It can only be achieved through the eyes of those who judge you. If you do achieve excellence, you can only maintain it through constant innovation—the right side of the pyramid. All of that—people who truly care and constant innovation—requires a common sense of direction, I-65, and in-touch leadership.

The famous management educator and author Peter Drucker passed away in 2005. His influence on the science of management, however, transcends his life. He spoke to the theory of management and the sound practical philosophy of achieving business success. He is the father of management by objectives. Drucker was particularly clear on one point: the pursuit of excellence is the only sound strategy.

Tom Peters's work and writings on management theory followed Drucker by more than thirty years, but he shared Drucker's belief regarding the pursuit of excellence. In his 1985 book, *A Passion for Excellence*, Peters gave us the basic outline for achieving it. Peters explained that only people who truly believe in customer care could reach the goal. Lip service alone does not count. The concern for customers must be genuine. It is a relationship in which you like your customers and they like you.

In the pursuit of excellence, you do not get to determine when, or even if, you achieve the goal. Excellence must be earned through the eyes of those who judge you—your customers. If you do reach the target in their eyes, you can only maintain that accomplishment through the other side of the pyramid: constant innovation—a relentless and continual change for the better.

Succeeding at both customer care and innovation takes a sense of common direction (I-65 North) and an in-touch leadership for which Peters said management by wandering around, MBWA, is an essential tool. When Peters wrote *A Passion for Excellence*, the modern World Wide Web did not exist. We did not have websites, blogs, online meetings, collaboration tools, or business-class instant-messaging systems. There was no social media, five-star rating system, or online customer reviews. Thus, Peters's observation that "Excellence companies" practiced management by wandering around (MBWA) to achieve an in-touch state and a sense of common direction. Today, MBWA is no longer the only essential tool for in-touch leadership.

Organizations now have a wonderful array of tools for staying in touch with team members and customers. Let's call these new tools MBCA (management by communicating around) and add them to MBWA for achieving in-touch leadership. Constant communication is the essential element of both MBWA and MBCA. When team members and customers have to start questioning an organization's direction due to a lack of communication, the battle is lost.

Communication is never a one-way street, and it must always be honest. It must flow in all directions, which includes communication to and from customers. It must be consistent throughout the organization from the top to the bottom of the organization chart. That can only occur when every member of the team is confident that he or she understands the concept of I-65 North and the organization's core beliefs—its rules of the road—for navigating it.

**Excellence must be earned through
the eyes of those who judge you.**

THE FORCE

Customers are the only source of revenue.

In *Star Wars*, the Force flowed throughout the universe influencing all things. In business, the customer is the Force. Customers—and customers only—produce revenues and decide if a business will have the opportunity for successful results. Customers are the only source of revenue. All else is cost! Above all, excellent businesses are customer-oriented. They ask and they listen. They like their customers and their customers like them.

Throughout my career, I have been exposed to a large number of enterprises of all types, and very few approach what the author Jim Collins (*Good to Great*) would call "great."

In fact, many do not even make it to "good." That includes those organizations where a lack of leadership has allowed employees to react to customer contact as a distraction or interruption. You have probably heard the joke, "This would be a great business if it weren't for the damn customers."

Among businesses where new customer acquisition requires setup, installation, and training, another type of dysfunction is common among organizations failing to make the grade. The rest of the organization resents the sales team because the leadership has permitted two inappropriate sentiments to develop. (1) Members of the sales team get the big money—commissions—while the rest of us do all the work. (2) They—the sales team—cause all the problems. They make promises we have to fulfill, or we take the heat for not being able to deliver as promised.

Often in such situations, the sales team is operating with total independence. Consequently, every sale is viewed as something being done *to* the rest of the employees when it should be considered a collective success resulting from organizational teamwork and coordination. The leader of such an enterprise has failed to create a customer-focused environment (one that understands that no opportunity to succeed exists without a customer).

The excellent business leader will create a team environment in which the sense of success, recognition, and benefits of sales accomplishments are properly shared throughout the entire organization. This is usually easy to accomplish in a small organization and, with intent and focus, can be accomplished in large corporations. Production, performance, and other areas of the business—even legal and accounting, for example—can gain a sense of ownership for marketing and sales results through communication and participation in the development of sales strategies on a macro level and for targeted accounts on a micro level. All players on the team, from telephone operators to mailroom employees, should be partners in serving the Force.

When I started Juris, Inc. in 1986, one of the first things we did was create the "bell tradition." Every time we added a client, a sales bell signaled the success. Adding a new client to the Juris family was not just a commission for the salesperson, it was a victory for the team. In fact, cash prizes were distributed to the non-commissioned members of the team every Friday in our company-wide meeting. The prizes were based on the number of rings that week. Some of the prize money was based on specific contributions to the sales effort and some went to winners drawn at random from the hat. A different bell rang when no customer had to wait for a return call from customer support representatives busy helping other clients. At the time, such things were unique, but like our "casual Fridays," similar traditions are now commonplace.

As Juris grew, team members spread out across the country working in remote and home offices. We had to find new ways to maintain the tradition of involving the entire team in our sales and service successes. Thanks to advancing technology, this was not hard to accomplish. Actually, it is a simple formula—communication plus recognizing people for their contributions. This does not happen, however, without leadership.

Only customers provide an opportunity for results, all else is cost.

INTEGRITY

Integrity comes from the top.

Integrity (truth, honesty, and purpose)—the leader has to have it and he has to expect it from everyone on the team. In business, integrity is about more than just "Don't lie, don't cheat, and don't steal." It is integrity of purpose—to meet the needs and satisfy the wants of customers.

Excellent companies do not manufacture products or provide services that fail to deliver on their intended purpose. They do not engage in false advertising or deceptive practices. Those are the givens, the have-to's, the ones enshrined into law. Excellent companies go further. They have customer care integrity. Customer care, treating customers as the Force, has to be deep-seated and sincere. People resent a lack of integrity. They know when you are just going through the motions. They know when surveys are self-serving rather than a genuine effort to improve customer satisfaction. It does not take long for them to figure out that a customer loyalty program is one-sided, all about getting *from* you and giving little in return—too many blackout dates, for example.

Almost every retail business trains its employees to ask the simple question, "Did you find everything you wanted?" Not many of those employees seem to care about the answer. Only a few take any helpful action in response to a negative answer from the customer. Those who do usually do little more than direct the customer to the service desk where the customer can continue to pursue the issue. In short, the organization's employees have been trained to go through the motions. They have not been freed, or authorized, to solve their customers' problems.

Even worse than the insincere question is the insincere apology, yet that has somehow become standard operating practice. Make a complaint or call a helpline and the company's representative is trained to say, "We apologize for any inconvenience." Often they do not seem to care. They seem only to be going through the motions and repeating scripted answers.

On the other hand, the leaders at Home Depot try hard to instill a genuine customer-care mentality among their team members with hassle-free returns and a cadre of employees spread throughout their stores with marching orders to ask and deliver. The next time you are in one of their stores, ask an employee where to find a particular item and then notice that they do not just say, "I believe you will find that item on aisle twelve." They say, "I think that's on the left side of aisle twelve about halfway down on the bottom shelf—*just follow me, and I will take you there.*" You do not get the feeling that you have interrupted their job; you *are* their job. That is integrity of purpose—to satisfy the wants and needs of customers. Home Depot may not be perfect, but you know they care.

The difference between sincerity and insincerity is simple. To achieve sincerity, you must free your team to act and empower them to serve the customer. It is not always easy to accomplish this consistently. You have to work at it continually. Weed out insincerity—replace "We apologize for any inconvenience" with "I will do everything I can to make it right or find someone who can."

Integrity of purpose is about satisfying the wants and needs of customers.

Common Courtesy

"The eyes are the windows to the soul."

The "CC" eyes in the above graphic stand for common courtesy. It is said the eyes are the windows to the soul, and the soul of an outstanding company is common courtesy. Name just one missing trait that would disqualify an organization from greatness. I don't think there is any contest. The answer is common courtesy. Many things separate great companies from the mix. However, no organization that achieves excellence in the eyes of its customers has done so if its people have failed to practice common courtesy. If customers are not treated with common courtesy, then when they have an alternative—and eventually they will—they will take it.

When it comes to common courtesy, details matter. If you tolerate the little slips, you encourage bigger lapses. Leadership has to be proactive and create an environment where nothing less than common courtesy is the standard. For example, I find telephone practices in most companies to be decidedly unfriendly. Aside from an organization's website, the phone is the dominant point of contact between an enterprise and many of its customers. It is an area where lapses in common courtesy are easily committed. Too often, phone calls are treated like interruptions.

While shopping in Pike Place Market in Seattle, I came across the kiosk of a woodcarving artisan. He was selling small handmade mirrors perfect for a desk or workstation. This sparked an idea, from which I started a new tradition. From that day forward, every employee had one of these handmade mirrors by their phone. My message was "Our customers can hear a smile over the phone."

A leader creates the standard but also has to back it up with action. He or she must hold people accountable. I always include some real-life management issue in my mysteries. In my novel *The Claret Murders*, one of the characters is a jerk—the office bully. The leaders of his firm tolerate him because he brings in most of the new business. Their answer to complaints about him: "That is just his way. Don't take it personally." Well, people do take it personally. Stanford professor Robert Sutton spelled it out in his popular 2004 *Harvard Business Review* essay, "More Trouble than They're Worth." In his book *The No Asshole Rule*, he expanded that essay to expose the cost and consequences of office bullies. Office bullies are more than nuisances; they are serious and costly threats to employee morale and business success.

As you might guess, in *The Claret Murders,* we killed him—problem solved! In real life, you can't kill your bullies, but you cannot live with bullies either. You have to fire them and anyone else who fails your zero-tolerance tests for common courtesy. Office jerks are at one end of a line of negative behavior that includes unpleasantness, aloofness, rudeness, foul language, telegraphed feelings of superiority, and an "I'm too busy" attitude. It is a line devoid of common courtesy. Such behavior is a barrier that customers, vendors, other employees, and new recruits do not want to cross. The excellent leader will not make them cross it. He or she will have a zero-tolerance policy when it comes to common courtesy—"You can't work here without it. Period."

The soul of an outstanding company
is "CC": common courtesy.

LEADING EDGE

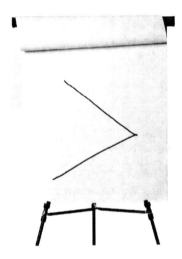

**Excellent companies are out
front—on the leading edge.**

The above chart represents the competitive position of a product or service. You can be on the leading edge or point, working to get there, or falling behind. Peter Drucker believed that only a leading-edge position allows a business to achieve long-term results. Anything less is at best competent, which leads to marginal. Taking a lead position with respect to a product or service does not have to mean bigger or more costly. It does mean an advantageous difference in the eyes of the customer. Excellent organizations pursue leading-edge positions by asking: *How can we remain different and better?* The effective team is constantly asking that question.

Getting out front with a leading-edge position is also an invitation to be persistently pursued because lead positions are both transitory and targets for the competition. It is a game of leapfrog. The excellent organization is constantly leapfrogging other leapfroggers to regain a new leading-edge position and stay on the cutting edge of their business.

Maintaining a leading-edge position is not a periodic task. It is a mind-set, one of constant innovation. You and your team are continually asking how you can do things differently—better, for less, faster, more conveniently for the customer, etc. You do not just ask within your organization. You ask customers, prospects, former customers, and prospects you lost to competitors. You ask and you listen. You study your competitors, and you even study what is happening in other industries and with unrelated products and services. John Deere engineers had an "Aha!" moment when they realized that if spacecrafts could dock with a space station, they should be able to dock tractors with their accessories without the driver getting out of his seat and without muscle power, wrenches, or screwdrivers. They made it work.

Maintaining a leading-edge position requires constantly questioning traditions, policies, and procedures. For example, if you are an innkeeper, you should be asking why hotels need to set check-in and checkout times—especially since car rental companies eliminated similar requirements years ago. What conditions dictated the check-in and checkout policy? Do those conditions still exist? If they do, can they be changed?

Finally, never forget that lead positions are different positions from the rest. They are a value unique to you. Can you answer the question, Why should a prospective customer pick us? Maintaining a leading edge starts with the answer to that question and the knowledge that, for long-term purposeful success, soon you must answer it differently.

Excellent organizations pursue leading-edge positions by asking, How can we remain different and better?

Fix It Before It Breaks

If it isn't broken, it is in the process of breaking.

As the image of the mechanic's tool and the words "Fix It" implies, everything is in the process of breaking. You have to fix things *before* they break. The notion that excellence, once achieved, can be maintained only through constant innovation and change brings us to the second certainty—change is constant.

The old saying "If it ain't broke, don't fix it!" is wrong because things are always in the process of breaking. Nothing is exempt. Everything—a chair, a desk, the technology on which you depend, the materials you use, the availability of labor, capital, competitive conditions, government controls, and customer preferences—is in a state of flux. Everything and every condition—whole industries, even human life—has a life cycle. Envision the following bell-shaped curve:

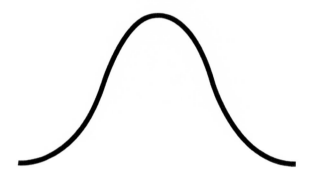

Things come into existence. They mature and prosper. They wane and begin to decline. Ultimately, they are replaced.

An organizational understanding of the life cycle is needed for long-term success of an enterprise. The survival of a business will depend on its leadership's ability to transform the business to avoid the decline and death predicted by the pattern of the bell-shaped life cycle curve. That transformation will only occur if leadership has instilled the concept of *fix it before it breaks* across the rank and file of the organization. How do you do that as a leader? By paying attention to the small things.

Rudy Giuliani will always be considered "America's mayor" for his leadership following the events of 9/11. Many of you, however, may not have experienced pre-Giuliani New York City. It was not a pretty sight. I remember walking toward Times Square. It was a cesspool overrun with crime, sex shops, and peep shows. XXX advertised the adult content and activity behind the storefronts, and as I passed by, I was propositioned repeatedly with sex and drugs. This was not a city to be proud of. Then Giuliani went on a campaign to eliminate broken windows in the city.

There are arguments, of course, about how much credit Giuliani should be given for the city's turnaround. In addition, debaters question the exact tools and conditions that enabled him to revitalize the Times Square area. There will always be those who want to diminish the power of leadership. However, I was there. It all started when Giuliani decided enough was enough—when he decided that decay and broken windows would not be tolerated. He used the power of zoning laws to bear down as the transformation gained momentum, but it was his unwillingness to accept disrepair that started things moving. He understood that if you paid attention to the small things, big things would follow; and they did—upscale hotels, theme stores, and restaurants, among other things.

I also remember visiting a law firm in a major Southern city. The firm had tried and repeatedly failed to install a modern computerized business system. Our software was their fourth attempt. They had fired previous vendors, and the conversion from the law firm's manual system to our product was not progressing as it should. I entered an overcrowded accounting office to find one person sleeping at his desk in a room seemingly devoid of fresh air. Mismatched desks in disrepair and pushed together left little room for personal space. Chairs had broken backs and missing arms. Seat cushions were patched with tape. What I saw explained the prior failures and the current lack of progress.

When leadership tolerates decay and disrepair, they will not have a team committed to keeping the organization's products, services, or operations in sound and healthy condition. On the other hand, by being intolerant of disrepair even of small things, a leader continuously reinforces the concept of fix it before it breaks. As the Giuliani story demonstrates, it is a mind-set that spreads and the big things follow.

"If it ain't broke, don't fix it!" is wrong because things are always in the process of breaking.

LIFE CYCLE

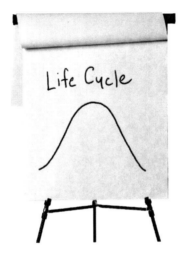

The need for your service or product the way you provide it is unlikely to continue to exist.

The life of a product or service, and, for that matter, everything else, is represented by a normal or bell-shaped curve like that above. Everything has a life cycle. If something exists, it is in the process of breaking. Things come into existence, peak, wane, and fade away. Things age, wear out, become obsolete, go out of style, etc. The successful company must always be asking: What is next? It must be engaged in strategic planning and intelligence gathering to map out its future—"fixing it before it breaks"—by moving across one life cycle to another. As one turns downward, the successful organization shifts its emphasis to a new life cycle—one beginning its upswing.

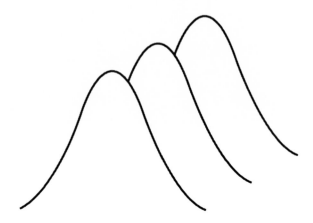

Think of the computer industry where room-sized main-frame machines were replaced by minicomputers that were then made obsolete by small desktop computers—personal computers (PCs)—that subsequently gave way to laptops, then tablets, and now smartphones. The evolution continues today.

Think of the remarkable reinvention of Apple by Steve Jobs as he moved the organization across multiple life cycles. Businesses that cannot or will not make the transition across life cycles fade away. The term *creative destruction* is often used to describe this remarkable phenomenon and the impact it can have, not only on individual companies but also on entire industries. Big-box stores wiping out small-town Main Street and the owner-operated independent hardware stores, drugstores, dime stores, and groceries. The music industry transitioned from 78s to 45s to 33rpm, then 8-tracks, cassettes, CDs, and now to digital.

Enterprises exist to deliver value and solve needs. For you as a leader or entrepreneur, it is essential you possess—and communicate—the sense that you do not exist to provide the service or the product that you currently offer. You especially do not exist to deliver it in the form or the way in which you do so today. *You exist to deliver value and fulfill needs.* You must evolve as abilities, needs, and expectations change. Sometimes your future will involve delivering value and fulfilling needs for which, at the present, your potential customers have not even been searching. That can be because they never imagined such a future thing could be invented. Often it will be because one new thing creates the need and desire for other new things.

The maturing of one life cycle and the introduction of its replacement is often a naturally occurring phenomenon. One that can be anticipated, planned for, and managed in an orderly fashion with the maturing life cycle financing the development of its replacement. The most profound influence that can alter the life cycle of an existing product, service, or entire industry is creative destruction. While the economic concept can be quite complex, in simple terms, *creative destruction* means "a newly created thing destroys its predecessors." Creative destruction can shorten one life cycle and create a host of new ones almost overnight. It is not easy to anticipate, and entrenched incumbents often underestimate its impact and fail to alter their economic model in time to survive.

The publishing industry is a perfect example of creative destruction. The old model of agent-publisher-distributor-retailer-library peaked somewhere in the past, and now due to new processes, it is on the downside of its life cycle. A new model brought on by an increasingly digital world has been taking over. The survivors in the book community will embrace the change and reinvent what they do and how they do it. They will shift from the downward path of the old print model's bell-shaped life cycle curve to the upward climb of the new digital life cycle that is gaining momentum. Legacy publishers and literary agents who fail to evolve new business models in harmony with the move to on-demand printing, eBooks, and self-publishing will perish. Brick-and-mortar bookstores will go the way of the bankrupt book retail chain Borders if they are unable to remake themselves in a world where more than 60 percent of printed books are already purchased online and where, in many instances, digital books are outselling printed editions.

Achieve long-term career and business survival by building one life cycle on top of another—new technology, new processes, new materials, and new ideas.

Continued existence of an enterprise depends on the timely transitioning from one life cycle to the next.

MOORE'S LAW

**Moore's Law is an uncontrollable rate of
decay in the value of existing things.**

The conventional concept of Moore's Law is that the power of technology doubles about every two years, but there is a worm in the apple, so to speak. Existing technology is like the apple in the graphic. Moore's Law is like the worm inside eating away at its flesh. Moore's Law means that for existing technology there is an uncontrollable rate of decay in economic values.

Technology is so embedded in products and services today that the reach of Moore's Law extends deep into our economic system, shortening the life cycle of any given product or service. The consequence is that the long-term economic value of any given thing—product, process, or service—is near zero. The enduring value of a thing is in its ongoing capacity to evolve—moving from one life cycle to another. Without that capacity to continually improve and replace, it will have a short life and quickly wind up in the graveyard of outdated ideas, products, and companies.

In the mid-'60s, when I began my career as a CPA, having intangible assets on a balance sheet was not a good thing. Bankers deducted goodwill and other intangibles to arrive at "net tangible book value." The financial world was all about hard assets and discounted cash flow. Your business was worth its hard assets and some multiple of its profit stream. Today some of our most highly valued public companies have no hard assets to speak of, and some have yet to earn a profit. Perceived value is increasingly concentrated in a company's intellectual property. There is real danger, however, concerning the preservation of that economic value.

We understand the productive life of a brick-and-mortar building. But what is the life of highly valuable intellectual property? Investors who approach the value of intellectual property on the same level as traditional hard assets with predictable lives are in for a rude awakening due, in large part, to the destructive aspect of Moore's Law—that worm eating away at existing values. It is not the current state of a company's intellectual property, but the company's capacity to maintain, evolve, and innovate that determines the real long-term value of a business.

Moore's Law is based on an observation made in 1965 by Gordon Moore, cofounder of Intel. He observed that the number of transistors per square inch on integrated circuits had doubled every year since the integrated circuit was invented. Moore predicted that this trend would continue for the foreseeable future. In subsequent years, the pace slowed down a bit, but data density still doubles approximately every eighteen months. As price falls and capacity increases in the future, the value of previously existing technology declines.

I have admittedly stretched the application of Moore's Law to convey its more general influence now that technology has become a direct, or indirect, component of most goods and services. Moore's Law focuses on the engineering and manufacturing of integrated circuits, but it follows that as integrated circuits go, so goes the products, processes, and methods that depend on them.

The view of Moore's Law as an uncontrollable rate of decay in the value of existing things is an important concept. It explains why the economic value of an enterprise, or its loyalty bond with its customers, is increasingly related to its capacity to innovate and evolve. Value rests in the capacity to stay current and competitive, rather than in the tangibility or current state of existing products or services.

Given the uncontrollable rate of decay due to Moore's Law, long-term economic value rests entirely on the ability to evolve.

PARKINSON'S LAW

Work expands to fill available time.

As illustrated by this flip chart graphic, according to Parkinson's Law, we are in the constant process of becoming overworked and underpaid. That is because without intervention, work creates work, filling available time and driving expenses skyward to an unsustainable level.

The life cycle explains one of the natural forces at work driving change, but there are other factors at work as well. Parkinson's Law is one of the more important of those natural forces affecting business negatively. Cyril Northcote Parkinson (July 30, 1909 – March 9, 1993) was a British naval historian and author of approximately sixty books, the most famous of which is his bestseller *Parkinson's Law*, which established him as an important scholar within the field of public administration. He is credited with the observation that "work expands to fill available time" and by extension, "expenses rise to meet income." It is the idea that work creates work and thus management must be constantly diligent and alert—simplifying and eliminating. That is the ability that governments and other bureaucracies seem unable to master. Without change dedicated to simplifying and eliminating, negative forces will drive a business into unsustainable levels of inefficiency.

You do not have to look far for examples of Parkinson's Law. Consider those piles of printed reports. It seems that someone is always coming up with some new report. While new reports are added, old reports are seldom eliminated. Think about it. Someone has to prepare them, print them, and distribute them. Even if you have advanced along the technology scale and eliminated printing, the data still has to be recorded, collected, assembled into a usable format, and loaded into the organization's intranet or distributed by e-mail. They still expect people to read, digest, and analyze the information, printed or digital. Every report—new or old, useful or not—creates work and depletes available resources. The same is true of rules, policies, and procedures. Unchecked, they become cumulative, creating work and consuming resources. Management, therefore, must be constantly simplifying and eliminating. Without doing so, work will expand and expenses will rise to unsustainable levels.

Without intervention, expenses rise to meet income.

MANAGEMENT JUDO

Five weaknesses that can take your competitor—or you—down.

Peter Drucker identified common behavioral traits among established organizations. These traits gradually render the organization competitively weaker and give the alert company the opportunity to achieve increased market share through management judo—leveraging off the competitor's weaknesses for an advantage. The weaknesses that companies tend to develop include:

1. A "not invented here" (NIH) attitude that will make the company slow to take advantage of new technologies, processes, or materials, etc.

2. The "Creamer" will concentrate too long on the higher profit, upper end of the market, leaving the door open for others to enter the market through the lower end.

3. Failure to stay in touch with clients will result in the company emphasizing *its* idea of best quality or features ("Wrong Quality"), leaving the customer's real wants unsatisfied or the price too high.

4. The "Premium Pricer" is the high-priced alternative that continues to maintain or even increase price in the face of equal or superior competitive alternatives.

5. The "Maximizer" keeps adding features to satisfy marginal market elements. This leaves the door open for the niche company that will provide a simpler, lower cost product or service that only addresses the needs of a particular market segment.

It is important to understand that these same weaknesses will develop within your own organization without constant management effort.

The excellent company should be on the lookout for an opportunity to gain market share through management judo. Just as important, it should also be alert to the rise of any of those five weaknesses *within itself*. The seeds exist within any enterprise. Without watchful management, they will sprout, grow, and take hold. Where they do, the organization will lose market share and eventually fail.

A classic illustration of the maximizer influence is the rocky evolution of the consumer camera market. It started with the inexpensive one-button Brownie by Eastman Kodak, but evolved into the expensive 35mm camera loaded with options, features, and new adjustments designed to satisfy the desires of marginal segments of the possible market. Eventually, we saw the reintroduction of the one-button camera that satisfied 80 percent of the market—the segment that had become frustrated by expensive and burdensome adjustments and controls. Of course, the one-button camera had evolved from its Brownie days. The reintroduced one-button models were high performance devices. The evolution has continued and now merged with the digital revolution and smartphones.

The successful company must always be on guard against developing the weaknesses identified by Drucker. At the same time, it will remain alert for opportunities when its competitors fall into the behavioral trap—Drucker's five weaknesses.

The five weaknesses are part of the natural changes that pull an organization down unless it is purposely changing to improve.

Section II

CHANGE:

THE PATH TO EXCELLENCE

THE CHANGE CURVE

**To manage change, you have to
know what it looks like.**

The change curve drawn on the flip chart illustrates that change creates an initial sharp downward spike in performance or benefit. Performance or benefit only turns upward to achieve the targeted benefit over time.

Business success occurs through change. The organization seeking purposeful long-term success pursues excellence and leading-edge positions. It practices constant innovation. It diligently simplifies and eliminates. It practices management judo and guards against developing weaknesses internally.

The organization that does not do these things is at the mercy of the natural forces that change us for the worse.

Another TV commercial comes to mind here. The commercial shows a harried office receptionist trying to handle incoming phone calls. She says, "They told us that this new phone system would make everyone more productive." There is a long pause. She looks into the camera and says, "If you ask me, they have just made things worse."

To understand why things got worse, you have to know what change looks like. We make changes like the new telephone system because we immediately want to achieve a higher level of performance or benefit. In the real world, that is not the way change behaves.

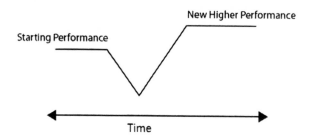

Change first creates a sharp *downward* spike in performance—the bigger the change, the bigger the downward spike. The less investment made in preparing for and managing change, the bigger the downward spike. The change curve turns upward only over time, and the rate of the upward climb is dependent on how effectively the change is managed.

Understanding the behavior of change, being able to visualize it as the above pictograph, is the first step toward being able to accept and manage change—one of the two certainties of life and business.

Visualize change to accept and manage it.

Managing Change: KASH

It takes KASH to stop the downward spike of change.

KASH is an acronym for the four things necessary for change to achieve its objectives. In order to stop the downward spike of the change curve and begin moving upward to achieve the targeted higher performance, those involved must have four things: new *Knowledge* combined with the right *Attitude* to acquire the necessary *Skills* that through use become *Habit* (KASH).

The people affected must acquire new knowledge. For the sake of illustrating what I mean by new knowledge, think of a user's manual or employee training. The receptionist trying to deal with a new phone system has to be trained, and equally important, all the people in the office need to understand how their piece of the system works, including its new benefits and features. If they have been given that prerequisite Knowledge, or eventually dig it out themselves, then with the right Attitude they will acquire new Skills (the skills required to use the new equipment and features). They will know how, but until those skills become Habit, higher performance will go unrealized. It is only with time that those skills become habit, which causes the change curve to reverse its downward trend and turn upward from its lowest point (the Valley of Despair), to climb up to the desired higher performance.

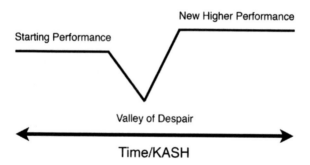

It is like an athlete who develops muscle memory. Taking advantage of the new equipment and benefits has to become instinctive. If you have to take the time to check with others, refer to a checklist, or open a user's guide, the new system will still be getting in the way of performance.

When a receptionist dealing with a new phone system says, "If you ask me, this has just made things worse," she is the victim of a lack of proactive change management. Sooner or later, in the example of the phone system, the organization will survive and get some of the desired benefit of upgrading its phone system—but not before hurting performance and frustrating its people and customers for some period of time. Other changes, however, left to fester similarly, can literally put a company out of business. Sadly, it is a scenario I have seen played out many times.

The ability to deal with change, to manage it or survive it, is significantly enhanced when you understand it. Visualizing its behavior—the downward spike, the Valley of Despair, and the slow upward movement—is enormously helpful. When they understand that the change curve turns upward because of KASH, managers are inclined to provide and foster it. Those affected by it seek out the needed new knowledge and are driven by a more positive attitude.

**We change to improve; it takes
KASH to make that happen.**

CHANGE GROUPS

**Rather than doing change *to* people,
involve people in the change.**

The graphic depicts a meeting—people working together. Forming groups among those to be affected by the change—to help plan and implement that change—creates ownership and commitment to it. It becomes *their* change rather than change being forced upon them, and thus helps to flatten the downward spike of the change curve and reduce its duration. One of the most important roles of a change group involves planning the content and form of the required new knowledge—training programs, instruction manuals, KASH books, one-on-one training, buddy systems, temporary or permanent help desks, and so forth.

There are few changes so small that their impact justifies ignoring the need for change management, and virtually all change involving multiple people will benefit from the use of change groups. Consider the impact of installing a new telephone system or something as simple as bringing in a new copy machine. A little advanced planning, disseminating the right knowledge in the right form to the right people, and ceremonialism (recognizing accomplishments, paying attention to it) can pay big dividends in terms of achieving the desired benefit without costly disruption and frustration.

Of the four elements of KASH (Knowledge, Attitude, Skills, and Habit), attitude is the most difficult to manage. A negative attitude—resistance to change—is reduced when people become a part of the change process rather than victims of it. Forming change groups helps create that sense of ownership.

One of the functions of leadership is education. That should include continuously reinforcing the organization's understanding of the previously discussed two certainties in life and business: change is constant, and we are always judged by others. If change is constant, everyone in the organization must understand the change curve and the important tools for change management.

Change groups create ownership of and commitment to the change.

HAWTHORNE EFFECT

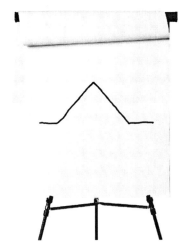

**Management can push or pull
against the downward spike.**

The graphic for the Hawthorne effect is an upward pulse that can push against the downward spike of the change curve.

The Hawthorne effect is one tool for minimizing the downward spike of the change curve. Management scientists found that increased attention alone improves performance even if only temporarily. Experienced leaders use drama and pizzazz to kick off change. They increase MBWA and MBCA (management by wandering around/management by communicating around) during periods of change. They set initial low goals and reward accomplishments. Daily, hourly, and even real-time progress reporting is used to celebrate milestones achieved.

While the Hawthorne effect flattens the change curve, reducing its downward spike, a word of warning is appropriate. Increased attention alone is not enough to assure success of change put in motion. Studies indicate that productivity often drops when the increased attention is withdrawn. Taking advantage of the Hawthorne effect is a useful tool, but it is only one of the tools for managing change. Along with increased attention, management must make sure that those involved get the right information and the support they need to acquire essential new skills, which will become habit through use.

The Hawthorne effect gets its name from the Western Electric factory outside of Chicago, where productivity tests were conducted in the late 1920s and early '30s. In more general terms, management scientists concluded that behavior changes when we are being observed. Thus, the Hawthorne effect is sometimes referred to as the *observation effect*.

Attention alone can flatten the change curve but only temporarily.

CEREMONIALISM

Nothing encourages success more than success.

W e all like to be recognized for our contributions and achievements. Effective change management looks for opportunities to provide an upward push against the downward spike of the change curve with awards and recognition tied to the KASH formula. Examples include:

- Certificates for completing training courses designed to deliver new knowledge

- Lapel pins recognizing milestone achievements

- T-shirts, hats, or jackets with goal-oriented messages reinforcing the purpose of the change

- Cash awards for individual or team accomplishments

Many weight loss regimes receive important boosts by early, quick weight loss. Setting initial goals that are quickly achievable and then recognizing their accomplishment reassures people going through a change that the change is working.

Reward early accomplishments to encourage success—it is all about pushing and pulling against the downward spike.

LIMITED RESOURCES

Resource availability is not the issue. Deployment is.

The image of an hourglass illustrates the fallacy of throwing money or other resources at a problem. Whatever you throw at the problem, it has to get through the narrow throat of the hourglass.

A profound influence on the downward spike of the change curve is the natural limitation of resources. Large changes have put many companies out of business. The depth and width of the downward spike becomes too big to overcome.

A recurrent example is that of a small company in a relatively fast-growing market that wants to increase sales results significantly. A new sales manager is hired (or worse, their top salesperson is promoted) and given the objective of doubling new account acquisitions. The plan seems simple enough: To double sales, double the sales staff.

Only the objective is never realized. In fact, if you double your sales force too quickly, sales typically fall through the basement. Why? It takes time for new additions to become productive. While new salespeople are not yet productive, the original salespeople are spending much of their time mentoring, training, and answering the new people's questions. Never forget Parkinson's Law: *Work creates work.*

Deploying new resources is work. Like it or not, new capacity actually decreases productivity until those new resources are deployed and fully productive. Do it too fast and you can put an organization out of business.

For an enterprise purposefully pursuing long-term success, there is no such thing as unlimited resources. It makes no difference if you have the funds to double the sales force, triple it, or quadruple it. It makes no difference if undeployed labor, capital, or material is available. Resources have to be deployed to become productive, and deploying them consumes existing resources and energy.

The concept of limited resources due to deployment is like an hourglass. No matter how fast you fill the top half of the hourglass, you still face the slow process of getting additional resources through the neck of the hourglass before they become productive.

Deployment, not availability, is the issue.

RELATIVE PERCEPTION

Does it always get worse after change?

Look at the two images on the flip chart above. Are they the same? No. The lower image has ten light spokes versus just nine on the upper image. The small change usually goes unnoticed.

The downward spike of the change curve is relative to the size, or even just the perception of the size, of the change. There are indications that the reaction to change is practically nil below a level of 10 percent. For example, a less-than-10-percent change in color, audio volume, or brightness of lights will go unnoticed, and thus there would be little negative consequences and little or no reaction to the change.

For another illustration of relative perception, consider the purchase of a new car. Let's say you are looking at a $40,000 car. The salesperson suggests you upgrade the standard radio to their deluxe model. The new price of the car is $40,350 and the increase in the monthly payment is only pocket change. It is an easy decision—a no-brainer. You opt for the upgrade.

What if you are purchasing a radio with no car involved? The price disparity would look entirely different to you. The standard radio model is $225. The upgraded model is $575. The relative change or difference in price appears significant, and your reaction to that change would be quite different—the decision to upgrade would not be as inviting—even though both instances have the same $350 difference.

Sometimes you can get there faster by going slower and making smaller changes.

INCREMENTALISM

Incrementalism

**Steps make sense—ever try getting to
the second floor in one big step?**

The graphic on the flip chart illustrates a series of small change curves, each with a shallow downward spike that forms a stairstep to higher performance.

The right way to implement change is proportional to the ability of the organization to deal with and absorb the downward spike of the change curve. In many cases, that will dictate the need to pursue the desired result through a series of incremental steps using the change management technique of incrementalism.

To illustrate the need to keep change proportional to the organization's ability to absorb the change, consider a successful restaurant that wants to expand. The owner decides to open a second facility across town. It is easy to imagine the downward spike in terms of performance and customer satisfaction at the existing facility as management's attention is redirected, and existing staff begins to train additional staff. Imagine the consequences when some of the best members of the kitchen and waitstaff transfer to the new facility. Doubling the organization requires a significant, hopefully short-term, negative investment that can put the business as a whole at risk.

Yes, there are things that can flatten the downward spike of the change curve and facilitate an early upward movement. Unfortunately, most small businesses making a similar move will fail to do those things, and their customers and wallet will suffer as a result.

Now consider the impact on existing facilities upon opening a third location. The organization's initial expansion has led to increased depth among its management team. There is a larger existing staff to draw from for the purpose of training new additions, and there is backup that allows some transfers to the new location without excessively cannibalizing the existing facilities. Opening a fourth location will have even less of a negative impact on existing facilities. With continued growth, the organization can develop and financially support people dedicated to the specialized task of project management involved in bringing a new location on board.

The larger organization spread over more and more facilities means that transfers have a smaller negative impact. As the base organization gets larger, the size of digestible incremental change increases. What makes the larger changes digestible is that each successive incremental change becomes smaller in relative size (the percent of change related to the base organization is smaller).

The undeniable conclusion is that the right way to make a change is to do it step by step—incrementally. However, is that always possible? For example, the growing food chain has to take that first big step—opening its second facility. Even there it is possible to find a way to break the project into incremental steps designed to minimize the downward spike. For instance, adding more staff to the original site ahead of time in small digestible steps, not after the fact. What about the added cost? If you cannot afford to do it right, do not do it at all. The consequences of failure are too great.

**Big changes should be broken down
into a series of manageable steps.**

CHANGE BY DECREE

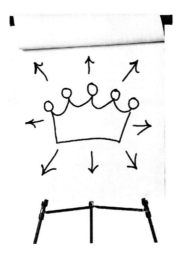

**"Do it because I'm the boss!" can result
in unpredictable outcomes.**

The change by decree graphic implies a royal, king-like action demanding change, and the arrows suggest the reaction to that demand could be all over the board.

If change is so risky and dangerous, one might conclude that it is something to avoid. The answer, of course, is that you cannot avoid it. Change is the very essence of business. Managed change is necessary to sustain any business. Unmanaged change, however, is unpredictable. It can have a positive or a negative impact. Likewise, external change that receives no response can reduce your competitiveness and can even eliminate the market for your goods or services.

Too often, entrenched market leaders ignore the changes occurring from disruptive technology or innovation. They focus on the "Wrong Q." (See "Management Judo.") For example, the Underwood company thought of itself as a typewriter company not as a company to help people produce documents. If they had changed their view of themselves and embraced emerging technology, they might still be around.

Survival requires businesses to respond to a constantly changing environment. Consider the chances of surviving in the music industry during the time when vinyl was displaced by cassettes and then CDs, which are now losing out to the downloading of digital songs. Consider what it was like to survive in the technology business as mainframes and service bureaus were replaced by minicomputers, which were quickly replaced by desktop computers—now under assault from the "cloud" and a host of handheld devices and tablets. How does one survive in the telecommunications field now that the Internet is here and thriving? How would you like to have been the leading manufacturer of fax machines? Consider the publishing industry now transitioning from the print age to the digital age. Long-term survival requires companies to embrace change, not avoid it.

We cannot avoid change, but we can avoid *unmanaged* change. That is why the wrong way to initiate change is by decree—"Do it because I said so!" or "Do it because I'm the boss."

Change by decree is unmanaged. It could be successful or it could fail. People do not react well to forced change, so one thing is certain: Whatever success is achieved, if any, will be achieved at a greater cost than necessary. Remember the icon for the condition required before the downward spike of the change curve is halted and turned upward—KASH. Change by decree does nothing to create a positive attitude or feeling of ownership, sabotaging the likely outcome from the onset. Unmanaged change endangers any organization.

"Do it because I said so" is unmanaged change and the results are random.

SLOT MACHINE MANAGEMENT

Every pull of the arm spirals the enterprise down to lower and lower performance.

Slot machine management characterizes another wrong way to make a change. The slot machine manager makes frequent changes similar to a compulsive gambler, repeatedly pulling the arm of a slot machine hoping the next pull will be a winner.

Change is essential for the long-term success of a business. Without change, success does not happen. The paradox is that the failure of management to understand change and competently manage it is high on the list of reasons businesses fail—not merely small businesses or new businesses.

Well-established businesses often fall victim to the lack of a corporate memory. Each generation of management tends to relearn the mistakes of prior generations. While their sheer size insulates giant corporations from disappearing altogether, they can wind up in the dustbin of wannabes—companies that are no longer in the leadership positions they once held.

The culprit is often a slot machine approach. IBM is one example. There was a period of time when the company reorganized frequently. They shifted managers to new roles and specialties before they had become competent in their current assignments. They realigned their sales force every six to twelve months—changing industry assignments, making regional and divisional reassignments. Each reorganization (each pull of the one-armed bandit) rendered the company less successful and less competitive—symptoms of slot machine management.

As performance declines, the slot machine manager reacts by implementing more change to stem the fall in performance. In effect, the gambler reaches up and pulls the slot machine handle with the hope that maybe this time he will hit the jackpot rather than lemons. That precipitates another fall in results and more changes by management, which spirals the company down to lower and lower results.

The compulsive gambler doesn't understand change and reacts with another pull of the handle.

JUGGLER EFFECT

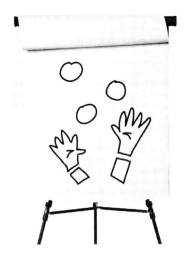

Personnel changes pose a special risk.

The graphic of hands juggling balls is a reminder that all of us are dealing with more than we can handle at a given time. We are juggling undealt with items until we can get to them.

Personnel changes—particularly those involving service, management, or professional positions—involve a special kind of risk that can have a strong influence on the steepness and depth of the change curve's downward spike.

All of us, in life and business, are like jugglers with balls in the air—approaching deadlines, uncompleted projects, unsolved problems, and unrealized opportunities. We manage our unresolved items against other priorities. When a change removes the juggler, letting those balls drop is the fastest way for a newcomer to start their tenure with a clean slate. They let the balls drop and lay the blame at the feet of the prior jobholder. The newcomer escapes blame, but the company still takes a hit (the juggler effect). Excellent companies do not let that happen. They identify critical or potentially damaging balls in the air and make sure the newcomer takes ownership or that an alternate plan exists for the orderly resolution of the juggled items.

To do otherwise creates unnecessary risk. In the absence of this aspect of change management, each personnel change exposes the organization to unnecessary risk. If no one is tending to the abandoned items, if no one has determined whether the juggled items are trivial or potentially damaging, the company's eye is "off the ball."

Leaving juggled items unattended may be of no consequence—or it may "unleash hell"!

STAR SALESPERSON

"All the world is a stage."

The graphic taken from the movie director's call "Lights, camera, action!" conveys the message that we are always onstage and that includes the business leader.

Low goals, ceremonialism, change groups, and the Hawthorne effect all depend on effective leadership. The best change managers are star salespersons. They add drama and pizzazz—they practice management by wandering around (MBWA) and management by communicating around (MBCA). They communicate in person, over the Internet, with posters, with T-shirts, in white papers, and in books and booklets.

They are the cheerleaders; however, they also have to do their homework. They understand change and they are prepared for it. They understand KASH: They determine the knowledge required and develop programs to deliver it. They understand the importance of attitude. They never force change. They do not utter the words "Do it because I said so." They involve those who will be affected by having them participate in the decision and assist in planning and managing the change. They reward accomplishing new skills and they stay involved, as needed, to assure that those new skills become habit.

Star salespeople are there from the beginning through the *Valley of Despair* (the bottom of the change curve) and the eventual climb to the targeted higher level of performance or benefit.

A little advanced planning, getting new knowledge to the right people, and recognizing accomplishments can pay big dividends in terms of achieving the desired benefit without costly disruption and frustration.

The best change managers are star performers—they add drama and pizzazz and "sell" the change.

Section III

MANAGEMENT:

GUIDELINES FOR EXCELLENCE

Management Cycle

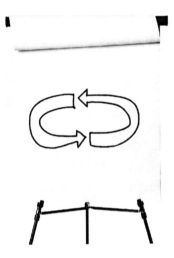

Modern-day jobs require management skills—a continuous process of pursuing objectives.

M anagement is about achieving objectives—be it at the enterprise, department, or individual level. It applies to all of life as well as business. It is planning, organizing, acting, and controlling. It is a continuous cycle of processing input, taking action, collecting feedback, and repeating the process. Nothing happens until something happens. When the action significantly affects the organization, its people, its processes, and its customers, it requires the specialized steps of change management. However, management is more encompassing and requires more tools and skills than just change management. Management is also not the same as supervision. Supervision may be involved in an individual's managerial role, but management is broader in scope.

While many modern-day jobs do not involve overseeing the performance of subordinates, they do involve a high degree of individual authority and accountability, which pushes those jobs into the management category. These are jobs where the individual must manage relationships with customers and with internally accessible resources and specialty areas to accomplish their assigned objectives. To do their jobs competently, these workers must plan, organize, act, and control—continuously processing input, taking action, collecting feedback, and then repeating the process—which is the definition of the management cycle. Thus, management concepts apply to these jobs as much as they do to those responsible for organizational groups, units, departments, divisions, companies, or broad-based enterprises.

Management concepts are important in life as well as business—they are about planning, organizing, acting, and controlling.

FIVE THINGS

What do excellent companies do differently?

The flip chart graphic is a reminder that purposely successful organizations intentionally do five things that set them apart:

1. Engage in the planning process

2. Set goals and objectives

3. Develop plans for achieving those goals

4. Prepare their team for opportunities and contingencies

5. Measure progress and hold people accountable

Any organized group of people and their endeavor or enterprise can be accidentally successful for a short period of time—they can have their Andy Warhol's "fifteen minutes of fame." It is even more likely, however, that they will simply fail without achieving any success.

Only a few organizational teams achieve excellence. In Jim Collins's vernacular, only a few go from good to great. As for the rest, either they do not plan at all or the "production of the plan"—a well-written and attractively bound document—has become the goal itself. The problem, of course, is that the best thought-out plan resting on the bookshelf serves its purpose about as well as a broken watch tells time—it shows the correct time twice every day. A general is said to have barked: "All plans are good until the first bullets are fired. Then it all goes out the window." The actual quote was probably more colorful.

Planning is an ongoing process. It is not some bound book. The plan shapes the decisions and actions of the team by establishing temporary targets—and the team's actions and decisions made on the front line change the plan.

It is a dynamic process. As time advances on the future, assumptions become more accurate. Decisions and actions made on the front line close in on a target that moves from a cone of uncertainty to a clearer target. For such a dynamic process to work, it must be a state of mind—a way of thinking and communicating—where the team is nimble and quick on its feet, constantly adjusting and refining the plan due to changing conditions and expectations.

The fifth thing on the list of distinguishing characteristics of a great organization is that it measures performance and holds people accountable. Holding people accountable is not all about penalties. Yes, people who mess up, who fail to achieve their objectives, pay a price and that can include job loss. The chief executive of a public company that woefully misses its target is likely to be on the job market. For the most part, however, holding people accountable means that recognition, advancement, and reward will depend on contribution not on tenure. It is all about achieving the objectives and goals established through planning. It is about successfully accomplishing the programs and steps designed to move the organization toward its objectives and goals. It is about successfully capitalizing on opportunities, dealing with threats, and contingencies. Great companies are meritocracies.

Only a few achieve excellence. Those who achieved excellence did five things differently, including planning and holding people accountable.

TEMPORARY TARGETS

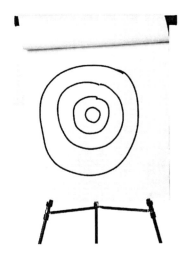

**Planning is doomed to fail unless the concept
exists that objectives are temporary targets.**

The future is uncertain; therefore, it would be folly to follow the plan at all costs! Planed objectives are targets
based on estimates about the future in view of current capa-
bilities and available opportunities. If planning is to work,
the "planning plan" must be to change the plan to fit new
circumstances.

As a young CPA, I was struck by a statement made by George
O. May, one of the early senior partners of Price Waterhouse
& Co. May said it would be impossible to determine the profit

or loss of an enterprise in so short a period as one year, if it were not necessary to do so.

Something like that can be said for planning. Assumptions about the future are too uncertain for sound planning purposes—except for the fact that planning provides an essential structure for the enterprise to react and adjust its actions for changing expectations about the future (making temporary targets).

The excellent leader's emphasis is on necessary changes to the plan rather than solely on the dogged pursuit of it.

**To plan without an expectation of
changing the plan is folly.**

COUNT THE TEETH

"Just the facts, ma'am."

Planning is not an intellectual forum for speculating about the determinable. The count the teeth icon is a reminder of the story about two Roman citizens debating the issue of how many teeth were in a horse's mouth. A poor knave overheard the argument. Tugging on the robe of one citizen, he said, "Sires, in yond field are two mounts. Why not count the teeth in the horse's mouth?" Whereupon they pulled their knives and killed the knave on the spot for upsetting their debate.

The excellent leader will insist that the teeth be counted, not debated. *Who* is buying our competitors' products and *why* are questions that counting the teeth can answer. Do not speculate! Count the teeth—do the research, ask the right questions of the right people.

There are too many meetings in the corporate world today and far too much time spent in those meetings speculating about the determinable. The instruction "Guys, just go count the teeth" is instantly understood.

Real facts and information rather than best guesses lead to better decisions.

ASK AND LISTEN

Excellent companies are all ears.

Another difference between a top-notch organization and the rest of the field has to do with listening. The excellent company is all ears, as illustrated by the graphic on the flip chart. It is an attribute developed among the organization's team by the leadership. An organization that truly cares about its customers has the curiosity to ask questions—and the sincere desire to want to know answers—all to benefit both parties. Asking and listening to the answers are hallmarks of great companies.

Consider this observation by Socrates: "Well, I am certainly wiser than this man. It is only too likely that neither of us has any knowledge to boast of; but he thinks that he knows something which he does not know, whereas I am quite conscious of my ignorance. At any rate, it seems that I am wiser than he is to this small extent, that I do not think that I know what I do not know."

The "all ears" ask-and-listen icon places emphasis on listening because it is the listening part that is a distinguishing characteristic of a great organization. Every organization asks questions. Many are not interested in the answers to most of the questions asked. We all get survey phone calls—ones where the recorded voice says, "On a scale of 1 to 10, how would you rank . . ." Then there are the surveys received through the mail with an attached donation request. Unfortunately, it often seems that no one is listening. Instead, survey questions are frequently asked in a way to influence you rather than to get helpful information from you.

Excellent organizations ask—and they listen. They are hungry for information such as: How are we doing, and how can we be better? What color would you prefer? Should it be smaller? What would have made it easier? What would have made you happier? They understand that excellence is earned through the eyes of those who judge us. They want to know how you think they are doing and what you think they could do better.

Asking is not enough—to get the answer, you have to *listen*.

SUBOPTIMIZATION

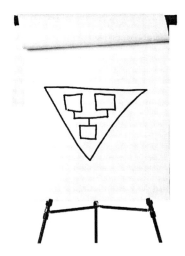

It is a case of the tail trying to wag the dog.

The upside-down organization chart represents a destructive development in the absence of effective leadership—suboptimization.

As an enterprise grows and begins to compartmentalize into specialized segments or departments, suboptimization (another natural negative change) will occur in the absence of strong leadership and frequent communication. Suboptimization is the condition in which a specialty area makes their own objectives a higher priority than the common objectives of the organization.

The tendency for suboptimization is a natural phenomenon and must be managed and controlled. Where conflict exists between the department's or unit's goals and those of the organization as a whole, suboptimization is damaging and distracting. For long-term purposeful success, the organization must be consistent and proactive in maintaining harmony between the goals of segments within the organization and those of the entire enterprise. Communication is essential to that process. Never assume that everyone knows the big picture.

A sales department's goal to reach a quota can lead to over-promising and under-delivering. The legal department's objective of protecting the firm from liability can result in one-sided and unrealistic terms. A shipping department's goal to avoid overtime can result in late deliveries to customers. The marketing department's goal for maintaining a uniform message can strangle the organization's efforts to reach diverse segments of the market.

By clearly communicating how each component of the organization contributes to the organization-wide goals, the occurrence of suboptimization is minimized. The team becomes aligned in pursuit of common goals with a clear sense of the strategies and tactics for achieving them.

The tendency for suboptimization is a natural one. Minimize it through communication and act swiftly to reverse it.

MEASUREMENT IMPROVES PERFORMANCE

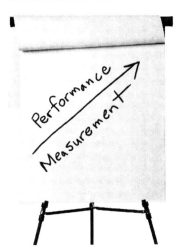

Measurement drives performance higher.

Excellent leaders are always out to "break records." Successively higher standards or goals result in successively higher achievement. It is the idea so frequently evidenced in the sports announcement, "It's a new record!" The most important set of measurements to develop are the organization's Key Performance Indicators (KPIs). These are the top-line metrics that must be achieved for the enterprise to meet its objectives. KPIs can be both financial and qualitative, but should be highly correlated with the top priorities of the firm and the firm's business model as developed during strategic planning. If there are more than ten KPIs, you probably have too many. That goes for the KPIs at the enterprise level or the KPIs for any of its supporting components or business units.

My son was part of the Colgate-Palmolive finance team from 1992 to 1997. He reports that they managed their entire worldwide operation with only ten Key Performance Indicators. The first thing every business unit's general manager would review when presenting to the CEO would be their results against those ten KPIs. They spent the rest of the meeting explaining how they achieved their goals or why they did not meet them.

I devoted a large portion of my career to working with law firms whose KPIs included such metrics as leverage, effective rate, productivity, realization, days to bill and collect, client intake, and closed cases. Whatever the nature of your business or organization, its success depends on certain things, and those main things should be the subject of your KPIs.

Excellent leaders are unabashed believers in the power of goals, and they know that successively higher goals result in higher achievements. They are always out to "break records."

Well-run companies set goals and continue to raise them.

ENCORE

"What's next?" is a reality of business.

The organization's leadership team must always be thinking, "What will we do for an encore?" Those who judge us expect successively higher results. Planners and managers must consider this expectation and exercise control to achieve it. It means "keeping your powder dry." It means not operating on the razor's edge. It means building elasticity into the business. It means developing early warning systems and gap planning to make up shortfalls. The encore expectation is not limited to financial performance. It includes product innovation, customer satisfaction, and other things.

**The curtain never falls; excellent leaders
are always working on the next encore.**

EVENT HORIZON

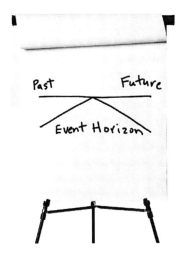

Keep your eyes looking forward.

The flip chart graphic illustrates that the event horizon in time is "now." It isn't about what has happened or what might happen; it is what is happening *right now*. It is sometimes called "real time" and it is an essential ingredient for in-touch leadership. You are not going to get where you want to be by looking in the rearview mirror. Great leaders want to know how they are doing, not how they did. The traditional tool for gaining that knowledge has been MBWA, management by wandering around. "Wandering around" meant you were in touch with your business as of a real point in time. You were experiencing, up close and in person, the event horizon.

The event horizon is a boundary in space and time beyond which events cannot be observed. It is real time. It is how things are *right now*. Until recently, except for personal experiences from MBWA, every other piece of information available to the traditional manager was looking backward. The leader in the late 1900s suffered from information overload, but all of it was out of date. Management had been at a disadvantage for centuries because their information systems only told them about past events. By the time the information got to the manager, it was too late to take any action that would change or improve the outcomes of events and transactions.

Times have changed. Management by wandering around has taken on an entirely new meaning. Now we can "wander around" through technology and social media. We can manage by communicating around (MBCA). The best companies are hungry consumers of technology that will put them closer to the event horizon. They use social media, blogs, websites, and cloud-based tools to have real-time contact with customers. They track, in real time, customer Internet reviews and comments about the company's products and services as well as the products and services of competitors. Using technology and wireless communication resources, excellent companies can and do operate at, and sometimes just over the edge of, the event horizon. Technology—including trend analysis, forecasting, real-time tracking systems, and social media monitoring—can show us what will occur if we fail to take action now to alter the future.

Information guides an organization to its targeted goals provided the information is timely, relevant, accurate, comprehensive, and navigable. Today's Executive Support Systems (ESS) do just that. They gather, analyze, and summarize the key internal and external information. They provide the modern executive with aircraft-cockpit-like command and control—with instruments showing the status of all key metrics necessary to "keep the plane in the air" and accomplish its mission. Great companies keep their eyes looking ahead and never go second class when it comes to technology that can put them at the event horizon.

Excellent companies are not satisfied knowing how they did—that is yesterday's news!

MANAGEMENT CANDY

It is about doing the right things the right way.

Management candy, M&M's, stands for **Main** things with **Minimum** resources. There are right ways and wrong ways to pursue objectives. M&M's, or management candy, represents the right way—doing the *Main* things necessary to achieve the objective with the *Minimum* resources required.

Management candy is an extraordinarily powerful concept that, once assimilated into the culture of an enterprise, alters how team members think and make decisions. It forces individuals, working groups, departments, divisions, and company leaders to ask and answer the following questions:

Main Things for Success: What are the main things my group's success depends on?

Main Strategies: What are the main strategies we will rely on to achieve the main things our success depends on?

Main Tactics: What are the main tactics we will use to implement our main strategies for achieving the main things our success depends on?

Minimum Resources: What are the minimum resources required for those tactics?

When these questions are asked and answered at the individual level, working group level, and the department level, you have an opportunity-focused team thinking and acting strategically. Few companies achieve that performance level.

Initially some people have a difficult time understanding the implications and importance of the notion of "minimum resources required." When people hear the word *minimum,* they tend to think you mean "on the cheap"—trying to get by with less than the optimum effort or resources—cutting corners, poor quality, and so on. Nothing could be further from the truth. In fact, using the minimum resources required means doing what is absolutely necessary to achieve the objective—*nothing less* but nothing more. In commonsense terms, "Don't use a sledgehammer to crack a nut."

The concept of using the minimum resources required is intended to convey that once we have achieved our objective, we will have a new objective and need resources to pursue that new opportunity. There is always an encore to be performed. There is always another mountain to climb. Conserve resources for future investment in the pursuit of new opportunities. Generals hold troops in reserve. Soldiers keep some powder dry. Excellent leaders use the minimum resources required to achieve their goals.

Management candy produces a culture of strategic thinking and decision-making. The *minimum* side of management candy does not encourage half measures. One of my favorite sayings is that "It only costs a little more to go second class." It costs more because of the do-overs, delays, and the wasted and frustrated resources. Make the investment that will get the job done. Then move on to the next project.

Great leaders focus on the main
things success depends on.

Rule of the Fewest

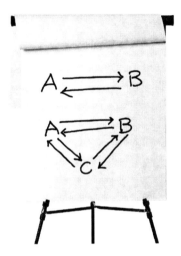

More is often not the answer.

Stretch the idea of Parkinson's Law, that work creates work, and you will gain insight into the importance of the rule of the fewest—a concept that reinforces and helps explain why management candy is so central to an organization's success. Consider the ease of internal communication in a two-person organization. As illustrated by the A-to-B graphic above, communication can only go two ways: from A to B and back again. What happens when you add a third person, employee C, to the team? The communication path increases from two to six different ways as illustrated by the following pictograph:

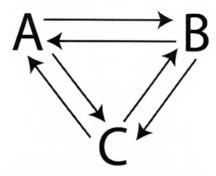

Imagine the increase in complexity when you add employee D, E, or F. The communication challenge eventually becomes so great that the business structure gives way to the customary hierarchical organization pattern with its own built-in inefficiencies.

The point is that people, relationships, and things introduce complexities that consume resources. The more things you have to deal with, the more inefficient the organization is in relation to its available resources. In other words, the more things you have to deal with, the more resources you must have to achieve a given result. Conversely, the fewer things you have to deal with, the easier it is to achieve a specific result.

As a business, you want no more products, no more pricing variations, no more prospects, no more clients, no more employees, no more dealers, no more locations, etc., than you must have to achieve your objective. Every complication, every unnecessary thing or variation makes managing more difficult and the organization less efficient.

Unnecessary things make achieving an objective harder.

Sunk Cost

What is done is done.

Sunk cost relates to what accountants call "relevant cost." It is the idea that what has occurred is not important to the decision-making process. For example, the original cost of a sunken ship is not relevant. That money is already spent. The cost of raising and reconditioning the ship versus the cost of new construction is the only relevant issue. If remaining costs are not justified, then no matter how difficult the decision, blunt realism provides the answer.

Unexpected events can lead to a need to change or abandon previous plans and ongoing projects. Excellent enterprises never bet the organization's future on the success of one plan or project. They act, test, react, adjust, and then move forward again. Egos and the human reluctance to walk away, however, can get in the way of making sound decisions.

You have heard the argument before: "We can't stop now; we've invested too much." When you hear that argument, it usually means that to stop a project or to change a plan would mean admitting a mistake. Admitting mistakes is what excellent leaders do. They minimize mistakes through planning and control, but when they occur, excellent leaders cut their losses, admit their mistakes, and move on. A leader uses such opportunities to disseminate and reinforce the concept of sunk cost within the organization. By doing so, he or she minimizes ego-driven poor decision-making going forward.

**Wise leaders are proactive opponents
of ego-based decision-making.**

PLAYBOOK

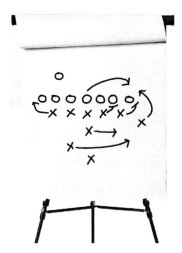

You need everyone reading from the same playbook.

The playbook illustrated in this flip chart graphic conveys that planning is about communication and coordination—command and control. The objective is to empower members of the team by giving a clear sense of direction and the rules of the road for getting there. The playbook equips members of the team to make the right decisions and take the right action on the front line.

Great organizations engage in the planning process, they set goals and objectives and develop plans for achieving those goals. They update those as conditions and circumstances change. To use a sports analogy, they prepare a playbook for team members and update it as they go through the season. To win, they need everyone working together. They need them reading from the same playbook.

In the commercial world, the playbook is not a three-ring binder. In fact, things move so fast today that if it is in print, it is already out of date. In this age of advanced communications and technology, an organization's playbook is the totality of the communication between the organization's leaders and their teams. That includes the leader's blog and tweets as well as the organization's website. It includes its intranet, extranet, and proprietary business system.

Regardless of form, the point is that the individual players need a playbook in order to perform as a unified team. Giving them that playbook means continuously communicating and reinforcing the organization's plans and core beliefs. Through that process an organization acquires its character, personality, or culture. It is the playbook that turns a group of individuals into a team.

The better the playbook, the better the team.

Section IV

OPPORTUNITIES:

STRATEGIES FOR EXCELLENCE

HEADING NORTH

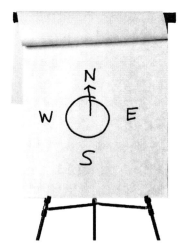

North has always guided man.

The flip chart image pointing north is a reminder that the excellent leader is a focused one—focused on a specific direction, one that represents opportunities. The North Star has guided explorers in search of new horizons. North is the important point on a compass. It conveys a sense of upward direction or momentum—a pursuit of opportunities. "We are going north—not south, east, or west." Excellent leaders are *opportunity focused*. They are not "problem solvers" or "risk avoiders." They pursue opportunities. That is why people want to follow great leaders. Opportunities are uplifting. They are meaningful and once achieved they make a difference. Opportunities are something people want to be part of.

The thing about problems is that when you solve one, there is always another waiting in the wings. Opportunities achieved add value; problems solved only return things to normal. So where are resources better spent? I have heard presidential candidates define themselves as problem solvers. I have interviewed many C-level job candidates who were quick to say, "I'm a problem solver." They did not get the job.

Success comes from recognizing and targeting the right opportunities. It comes from identifying the main things your success depends on, and adopting the right strategies to achieve them. Those are the things, not problem solving, that give an enterprise the chance to succeed. Of course, there are problems that have to be dealt with. Those will be covered in the section called "Problem Policy."

North defines the mind-set of excellent leaders—they have an opportunity focus.

ACRES OF DIAMONDS

All that glitters is not gold—or don't go elsewhere digging for diamonds until you have looked at home.

Russell Conwell, a minister and the founder of Temple University, may be most famous for his "Acres of Diamonds" story—the retelling of an old fable similar to the American folk saying, "The grass always looks greener on the other side of the fence."

In this story, Conwell tells of a man who wanted to find diamonds so badly that he sold his property and went off in search of them. The new owner discovered that a rich diamond mine was located right there on the property.

The things you must do to succeed in your current endeavor always look harder than something else you might do. If you are in the hamburger business, the pizza business looks easier and more profitable. If you are in the home-cleaning business, someone is going to tell you that you should change to commercial cleaning because it is easier and the money is better. If you sell to lawyers, you know the problems and difficulties of doing so. It is hard to get passed the gatekeeper, and once you do, getting a decision is a challenge of monumental proportions. On the other hand, if you were inexperienced dealing with accountants, you might think, "Surely, it would be an easier market."

Wherever you are, where you *aren't* looks better. At least it looks better to those who have not learned the lesson. Remember what Socrates said: *You don't know what you don't know.* Do not go looking for diamonds elsewhere until you first dig in your own backyard. As for grass looking greener on the other side of the fence, do not fall for it.

Igor Ansoff (1918–2002), considered by some to be the father of modern strategic thinking, developed a graphic matrix that visually illustrates the basic strategies for business growth and at the same time provides an easy explanation as to why the grass is seldom greener on the other side of the fence. Rather than greener, according to Ansoff, it is riskier.

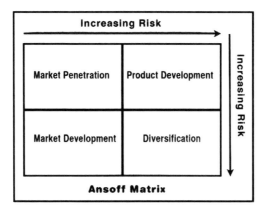

The matrix, which appeared in his 1995 book *Corporate Strategy,* illustrates the four basic strategies for business growth:

1. Market Penetration—selling more existing products into existing markets, usually by increased sales staff, promotions, pricing changes, or new routes to market (for example, online)

2. Product Development—developing new products or services for existing markets

3. Market Development—taking existing products or services to new markets

4. Diversification—developing new products and putting them into new markets

Market penetration involves digging in your own backyard. Risk increases when you embark on developing new products to sell to your existing market. The risk of failure really shoots up when you begin digging in someone else's backyard, attempting to transition your existing products to new markets, or to diversify with new markets and new products.

The moral of the story is *you don't know what you don't know*, so look for opportunities close to home (what you know) before venturing into the unknown.

LONG TAIL STRATEGY

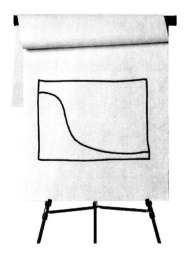

Shelf space no longer rules.

The graphic on the flip chart depicts the right-hand side of a bell-shaped curve, the so-called long tail. The long tail is a new economic model made feasible by technology that frees commercial enterprises from traditional constraints primarily related to the cost of inventory and distribution. The potential market of a commercial enterprise can be viewed as a normal or bell-shaped curve. The tail refers to that portion of the market where the potential volume of transactions is too low to serve profitably with tangible products and face-to-face services.

Because of the carrying and distribution costs, commercial enterprises traditionally have had business models influenced heavily by the law of disproportionate results—the 80/20 principle. In the brick-and-mortar world, 80 percent of results were traditionally derived from only 20 percent of the activity (sales, inventory, paperwork, jobs, shelf space, etc.). Management's job involved constant diligence to eliminate low yield or nonproductive activities. Unfortunately, that often meant a decline in service and a slow but relentless movement toward sameness. It was, as the American futurist Alvin Toffler predicted, a world of unlimited choices—all of them the same. You can have anything you want as long as it is within the 20 percent of alternatives that 80 percent of the population fits or prefers.

Futurist Alvin Toffler is perhaps best known for his 1970s book *Future Shock*. Reacting to the emerging digital age, he saw the future in terms of *information overload* and a move toward *sameness*. If we are lucky, technology may actually save us from the very things Toffler saw as its result. Through technology's ability to deliver information that is relevant and timely only when we need it, we are beginning to win against information overload. In addition, digital alternatives to tangible products and face-to-face services are making it profitable to reach low volume segments of the market—the market in the tail of the normal curve.

The 80/20 Rule is still important when dealing in tangibles, but the long tail that Toffler did not see coming is the new dog on the block when it comes to an economic business model. In the digital world, the right side (or tail end) of the bell-shaped normal curve goes to infinity without ever reaching zero. When the cost of maintaining inventory, handling transactions, and distributing products or services drops to near zero, the long tail of the bell curve becomes almost as rewarding as its center—the center that used to account for 80 percent of all activity.

Today, digitally you can have almost any song, any book, and any video even if long ago they disappeared from traditional retail outlets. Because of low sales volume, it was no longer economically feasible to keep them on store shelves. The long tail's benefits are not limited to previously tangible products. Services previously delivered face-to-face are being repackaged to deliver through digital technology. The long tail, for example, is already creating offerings that compete with on-campus university access. Benefits of and opportunities created by the long tail are just beginning to be realized.

Today's excellent businesses look for opportunities to operate in the long tail while being mindful of the 80/20 Rule in other areas. A product or service does not have to be digital to gain some of the benefits of the long tail. The key is to reduce the cost of maintaining inventory, handling transactions, and distribution. When these costs are reduced or eliminated, some of the long tail benefits become realizable.

The long tail opens ignored markets and gives new life to retired products.

BLUE OCEAN STRATEGY

Why keep swimming in the same crowded water?

The flip chart graphic of ocean waves represents the "Blue Ocean," the name of a business strategy for creative leaders who do not accept prevailing rules. They do not settle for "coloring inside the lines." They look for ways to reinvent how the wants and needs of customers and prospects can be satisfied. They look for opportunities to increase benefits that have gone unsatisfied. They look for ways to reinvent how they deliver products and services. There are successful businesses today that no one could have imagined a few years ago. Peter Drucker would say they created utility where there was none. Thomas Edison did that when he created the electric light, the phonograph, and moving pictures.

W. Chan Kim and Renée Mauborgne gave this strategy a name. They called it the Blue Ocean Strategy (BOS). According to Kim and Mauborgne, traditional businesses are "red ocean" businesses. In the red ocean, businesses compete with other businesses for the same customers to fill the same need. They compete in the same ways. It is a game of one-upmanship—for one business to gain market share, another has to lose. Businesses ebb and flow in the red ocean in terms of competitive victories and losses. In the red ocean, no business will consistently succeed. Leadership styles are transient. Successful strategies do not continue in perpetuity. Applauded leadership methods fail with changing circumstances. The red ocean is a place where victories are only marginal improvements.

Under the creative leader, a corporate team looks for opportunities to stop playing the red ocean game. They create a new market, a blue ocean, where they are the only player. It is the notion of reinventing the business, but kicked up a notch. For example, it is not a matter of simply reinventing how existing products or services are provided to existing consumers. Instead, it is a matter of reinventing how the needs and wants of those customers are satisfied *and* inventing ways that those who currently do not take advantage of a particular product or service can receive its benefits.

With the Blue Ocean Strategy, you reinvent the *market*, not just the business enterprise pursuing that market. You break out of the model where everyone competes for the same business.

A pure blue ocean is an entirely new industry created by bringing in neglected potential-customer segments by offering them a compelling buyer utility not currently offered anywhere else. Making the breakthrough to a pure blue ocean is not something every group—no matter how creative or how exceptional—will achieve. Nevertheless, the constant effort to turn the water blue is a mark of the excellent leader.

Imagine, for example, the impact of a question I raised earlier in the "Leading Edge" section of this book. What if a hotel or motel business broke away from the fixed check-in and checkout times? Why can't hotels operate like rental car companies—customers check in any time and check out any time? The fixed check-in and checkout time is an example of practices that become industry-standard practices but do not serve the customer. Practices that reduce the customer's benefits should be the enemy of the excellent manager.

PayPal, Stamps.com, Bazaarvoice, and the fitness chain Curves are notable examples of blue ocean companies. In addition, so was Southwest Airlines, the company that eventually changed how airlines compete overall. So were FedEx and Starbucks. Amazon has changed how people shop and read books. A creative telecom carrier in Africa is creating a blue ocean by launching products that allow mobile users to transfer money to other mobile users across all mobile telephone networks. Africa is a country where mobile devices, solar power, and wireless communication are transformative; and telecom carriers are in a position to bring brick-and-mortar-type services to the masses. The fact that most of the companies I mentioned now have competitors illustrates that no matter how blue the ocean, the sharks eventually move in and it slowly begins to turn red. By that time, however, the initial entry has usually secured the market and nearly locked it in.

Kim and Mauborgne's book, *Blue Ocean Strategy: How to Create Uncontested Market Space and Make the Competition Irrelevant,* is the product of years of research and collaboration with fellow faculty and students at INSEAD—the French graduate business school and research institute considered one of the world's best business schools. INSEAD is particularly known for its influential alumni, a global network of business intellect and power. Theirs is a book that deserves to be on your bookshelf.

Smart leaders ask, "What have we been overlooking?" They look for blue oceans.

RECESSION STRATEGY

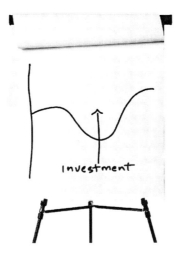

**Once the herd is gone, you have
the grass all to yourself.**

The flip chart graphic is an economic cycle and suggests that you should invest during periods of decline, that is, during recessions. Recessions are periods of opportunity for the prepared company. The sound recession strategy is a contrarian one—going against the herd: *Increase spending during recessions and stockpile "dry powder" during booms.*

The majority of businesses, including competitors, react to an economic downturn in the same way. First, they are usually unprepared. They immediately look for discretionary expenses to curtail. Investments in facilities and equipment go first. Employee travel goes next—including sales-related travel. Advertising, networking conferences, and trade-show participation follow quickly. In other words, they "hunker down" in defense mode.

Smart companies are not surprised by a recession. They understand that business cycles are a part of life. They do not suffer from a lack of corporate memory and have built into their strategic plans several tactics to prepare for and respond to economic recessions. While others curtail marketing activities, smart companies increase them, including advertising expenses. Rather than shrink their sales force, they snap up quality personnel laid off by others. Instead of canceling events, they increase their footprint at trade shows.

For prepared companies, recessions are bargain periods during which they can get the best deals for expanding facilities and adding or upgrading equipment and systems. Recessions provide one of the best climates for hiring top-notch people. It is a fertile time for building a network of consultants, independent contractors, dealers, and franchisees. It is a company's increased investment in marketing, however, that often pays off the most. Smart, prepared companies can come out of recessions with increased market share and financial strength.

The recovery and boom periods are best suited for consolidating gains and strengthening financial health and operational performance. During these periods, the excellent leader prepares for the next downturn by developing "dry powder"—emphasizing improved planning, workflow efficiency, and overall performance metrics. This is when you want to accumulate cash reserves and invest in equipment, systems, and facilities that will improve workflow efficiency and performance.

Many companies, most likely including your competition, respond to boom periods by overreaching and overextending. They increase financial leverage, deplete cash reserves, exhaust lines of credit, and max out borrowing power. When the next recession hits, they will have no choice but to conserve cash—and that means hunkering down, including drastically reducing marketing expenditures. Make sure you have a sound recession strategy in place. Make it part of your playbook to avoid the trap of overextending in good times and for taking advantage of recession-period opportunities.

Put it in writing: *We will avoid overextending during booms and will increase marketing and investments during bad times.*

MUSHROOM STRATEGY

**Acquisitions are like picking wild mushrooms.
Eat the wrong one, and it can kill you.**

The flip chart graphic of a field of mushrooms is representative of the risk involved in acquiring other businesses. Acquisitions can solve a strategic need but are a poor, sometimes deadly, growth strategy. Remember the saying "All mushrooms are edible—once."

A business has a personality—a unique culture. Even though a merger of two companies may appear to mean financial success, the clash of cultures often damages both organizations. There is a long-standing joke that being acquired is like being a mushroom. First, they put you in the dark. Then they dump manure on you. Finally, they can you. Unfortunately, there is some truth to the joke because eliminating people is the easiest way to cure the clash of cultures.

Even if an acquisition could be limited to acquiring a customer base, the square-peg-round-hole problem would still exist. The acquiring company finds its efforts redirected to assimilating clients who have chosen the acquired company's products or services for reasons that probably differ from the reasons the acquiring company's customers chose them. Their customers have different expectations and have relationships with the team of the acquired company that will be disrupted. More than likely, terms and prices will be different and must be blended together. It is likely that promises or expectations will complicate assimilation. Any way you cut it, resources and energy become redirected.

The encore expectation of the public often drives companies to play the acquisition game for continuing growth. The encore expected, if not demanded, is for companies to achieve successively higher results. Acquisitions usually follow a repeated pattern. The acquiring company consolidates operations by shedding people, which pushes profits up; however, with time the square-peg-round-hole disruption results in client or customer losses and declining profits. The acquirer makes another acquisition to achieve its expected successively higher results. Eventually the house of cards collapses.

One of the problems with going public is that the now-public company has a lot of cash *and* shareholders who expect that cash to be put to profitable use. The public company has little choice other than using its war chest to grow through acquisition. That, in turn, changes the nature of the business that attracted the new shareholders in the first place.

While acquisitions are a poor growth strategy, they can be a necessary tool to fill product or technology gaps or to provide a foothold into a new market. Nevertheless, generally speaking, they are high-risk, low-return alternatives.

The advantage acquisitions offer is immediacy, but immediacy comes with speed bumps that may slow you down in the long run.

Joining Hands

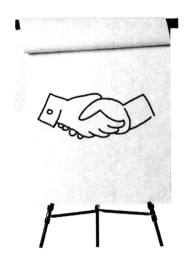

The power of people who like you is priceless!

The joining hands graphic represents the highest benefit-to-cost relationship an organization can have—a fan club! While acquisitions as a growth strategy are usually self-defeating in the long run, the low-cost-high-return character of leveraging off others—joining hands or getting a knee-up—to expand market share makes joining hands a common strategy among top companies, especially emerging ones.

Technology has eliminated the need for a nearby physical presence in many cases and created new opportunities for leveraging off others. For example, software companies certify independent trainers. Those trainers become promoters of the software. Social media has facilitated the creation of communities of users of a product or service.

A classic example of the community approach to joining hands is Harley Davidson. Today you can join an array of Harley groups—military personnel and veterans, female riders, African American riders, or the generic Harley Owners Group, better known as the HOGs. User groups and social media groups turn your clients and customers into spokespersons for your product or service.

DirecTV offers customers cash rewards for each new DirecTV customer they bring on board. The reward goes to both the referring customer and the new customer. DirecTV teaches its customers who are moving to a new home to take their equipment with them but to leave the dish behind. The tactic assures client retention and makes installation easier at both locations.

Excellent companies look for ways to leverage the power of others.

Do not confuse the notion of leveraging off others (joining hands) with dealers or franchises. The dealer and franchise business models are organizational tools related to brick-and-mortar business operations. When business growth requires physical outlets or "boots on the ground" near the customer, the dealer and franchise models are often sound strategies as alternatives to the capital-intensive alternative of company-owned outlets or remote staffing. However, they come with a price. Laws protecting franchisees limit the flexibility of the franchisor. Dealer agreements similarly complicate life for the mother company. The smart leader looks for opportunities to develop and foster non-contractual relationships and communities that advance and promote the interest of the organization.

**Excellent organizations are
recognizable by their fan clubs.**

RAZOR BLADE STRATEGY

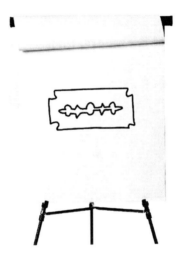

Blades are a lifetime need.

The razor and the razor blade represent an ideal business-to-customer relationship. A onetime event, the receipt of the razor by the customer, creates a continuing future need for a high-margin supplemental component, razor blades.

Entrepreneurs have used a classic three-step razor blade strategy to transform their moderately successful service business into a significant financial success.

1. Repackage the basic service in such a way that it can be marketed and priced like a product (the razor).

2. Add a high-margin component (the razor blade) for recurring revenue.

3. Add amenities to create a unique, high-value experience for the customer.

Likewise, a product company can be transformed by shifting its emphasis from a core product, the razor, to a related high-margin service or supplemental product, the razor blade. A second step is to make it easier for the customer to acquire the core product. That core product establishes the lasting relationship between the company and the customer, which in turn builds a growing demand for the company's high-margin supplemental component. Ideally, the product company will follow the lead of the service company by adding amenities to create a unique, high-value experience for the customer. This last step, if it is accomplished, insulates the company from pure price competition.

Printer companies are examples of product companies that have implemented the razor blade strategy. They have dramatically reduced the selling price of printers in favor of recurring high-profit ink and toner sales. The ink has low inventory and distribution costs when compared to hardware costs.

We also see manufacturers of coffeemakers shift from relying on the profitability of the equipment to the revenues produced by selling the coffee used by the coffeemakers— the coffee having a lower inventory and distribution cost. Clever coffee companies have also transformed their business by selling coffee systems and coffee clubs. They add exclusivity, deluxe packaging, and exotic blends to provide a unique customer experience.

Why is it important to create the "blade" component for your business? Pure product companies have to resell their product every year to produce revenues. In effect, the top line on the income statement of the product business starts at zero on the first of every year. The top line of the blade-orientated company is cumulative from year to year. Each year's new client additions add to the built-in recurring revenue line. With the blade component, new client sales are not the only source of revenue for a company. The existing client base provides a locked-in revenue stream. Razor and blade companies do not start from zero each year.

The excellent leader is a restless one. He or she uses transformative strategies to move from one life cycle to another, and they employ strategies like the long tail, Blue Ocean, and razor blade for a competitive advantage and increased results.

Razor companies have a sale; blade companies gain a relationship.

LUCK FAVORS THE PREPARED

Be Prepared!

The Swiss Army look-alike knife in the flip chart graphic represents being prepared to handle the unexpected. The versatile knife is the make-do tool for handling whatever confronts you.

Change (especially uncertain change) is the stuff of opportunities—provided you have developed a way of thinking that prepares the business to take advantage of whatever the future brings. French scientist Louis Pasteur said it in one short sentence: "Chance favors only the prepared mind."

When consulting with a midsize law firm a few years ago, I suggested that the partners adopt the practice of meeting monthly for a half-day session where they did nothing but think about things that could happen. The mission would be to identify strategies that would allow the firm to benefit rather than suffer from these events.

- Suppose the US government adopts a single-payer health system.

- What problems and opportunities would occur if Mexico were to nationalize American businesses?

- How would the firm respond to another Enron situation?

- Suppose a major client of the law firm contemplates moving its headquarters to a state where the firm currently does not practice.

- Is the firm prepared for the next Katrina?

- Does the aging of the baby boomer generation open opportunities for your firm?

With practice, could the firm have anticipated the events involving big tobacco, the rise of the overnight letter business, the advent of Amazon.com, or the wave of refinancing sparked by falling interest rates? Practice prepares a business team to take advantage of events that may surprise others.

Chance, luck, opportunities—whatever you call it—can best benefit those who are prepared.

COMPLETION RULE

**The last percentage of any project
carries the greatest risk.**

The rule for completion is that a project is ready for initial release when 80 percent of the design is 100 percent finished. Okay, I admit it. The 80 percent part is more of a guideline than a rule, but the concept is sound. This does not mean that a project or product should be delivered in an unfinished condition. It means that new ventures should be broken into phases. The initial delivery phase should normally contain only 80 to 90 percent of the tentatively planned full-release features. The initial version should nevertheless be fully finished—100 percent complete—with respect to the contents of that release.

Why stop at something less than the tentatively planned full design? First, no matter how hard you try, any project or development of significant scope is going to have some element of design or design implementation that falls short. The earlier you can release or deploy the new thing, the sooner you can identify market acceptance and discover needed changes and desired additions. Second, an early release also minimizes cost. It is always that last percentage of any project that consumes the most cost, adds the most complexity, and requires the most development time. Let those remaining items be the encores that the market expects from ongoing enterprises.

The acronyms QTP and SFS, which stand for "Quick-Turnaround Projects" and keep it "Short, Fast, and Simple," provide sound advice. While there are exceptions (Steve Jobs), excellent leaders do not "bet their companies." While Jobs and Apple won their bet—more than once, I should add—that kind of luck is extremely rare.

Excellent organizations pursue opportunities, not luck. They are not gamblers playing the sweepstakes. They practice constant innovation, but minimize the risk by following a pattern of "Act-Test-Act." They break big projects into smaller pieces to keep it simple so as to benefit from quick-turnaround projects. They test concept, design, and market acceptance as early as possible. They observe the completion rule.

Lower risk by reserving high cost, high complexity items for the expected encores.

CIRCLE OF SECRECY

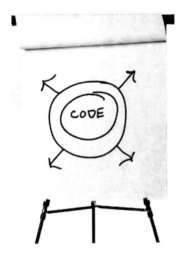

Two can keep a secret if one of them is dead.

The flip chart image of an expanding circle with a code name at its center is an illustration that, while you cannot keep a secret, you can manage the rate of expansion in the circle of those who know it. Code names are one of the management tools for managing the expansion of the circle of secrecy.

During the pursuit of certain opportunities, secrecy will become an issue. There are times when premature communication would be damaging or would jeopardize an important event. Acquisitions, new product development or releases, major reorganizations, significant price restructuring, and opening or closing a facility are examples that might warrant steps to avoid premature communication, especially during periods of preliminary consideration or planning. Nevertheless, no matter how hard you try, the circle of those who know something continues to expand until it becomes public knowledge. Therefore, rather than "keeping secrets," the tactic should be one of managing the circle of secrecy. Using a code name is an important tool for doing so.

The existence of a code name is a constant reminder of the sensitive nature of the information. Code names allow reference to an event or activity without giving away its nature. As time passes, more and more people become part of the circle of secrecy. The code name reinforces their obligation to protect confidential information from those outside the circle until the appropriate time for the information to become public knowledge.

In addition, as people enter the expanding circle, they may be brought into the fringes of knowledge by receiving only partial disclosure. To maintain integrity, they must know that they are receiving only limited facts—they are not receiving the whole story or the final story. The code name helps in that regard. It implies an obligation on their part to accept the incomplete information without attempting to uncover other details.

When public disclosure is about to occur, every effort should be made to first communicate it fully to the organization—to make every employee a member of the circle of secrecy. The team members who are becoming part of the expanding circle for the first time also need to know why the information was not divulged earlier. Excellent leaders do the following:

1. Refer to the event by its code name

2. Explain the reason for avoiding premature disclosure

3. Go over the timeline leading up to the current disclosure

These three steps are important for maintaining the integrity of ongoing communication. Rather than exclude employees, the steps provide a way of bringing everyone into the circle as soon as the leadership can do so.

If it is not possible to disclose to the team before a public announcement, carry out the same three steps in a team-wide event held separately but simultaneously with public disclosure.

Excellent companies practice constant communication that is honest and sincere. When communication is missing, it can lead to destructive alternative communication systems, such as the grapevine, rumor mill, and boss interpreters who explain what the company "really" meant. It follows that when there is an attempt to withhold information, it must be done with great care to avoid the loss of integrity. In that regard, it is helpful for the team to understand in advance how those situations are managed. How the organization handles its secrets should be covered in its playbook.

Management cannot keep secrets, but with the knowledge of their team, they can manage the timing of disclosure.

PROBLEM POLICY

Not all problems need to be solved!

The graphic image of a sign announcing the company's policy for dealing with problems is simple. We have a no-return policy—so if you take on a problem, you need to solve it! Do not just treat the symptoms because we do not accept having to deal with the same problem a second time.

Problems constantly confront business leaders, but the best leaders devote most of their energy to pursuing opportunities. Solving a problem merely restores things to normal. It adds no value, whereas the successful pursuit of an opportunity does. If management is going to concentrate on opportunities, it must carefully select the problems that will be solved and then deal with those problems in such a way that they will not have to be dealt with again. To do that, they have to peel back the skin of symptoms to find its core—the real problem.

Excellent leaders believe in the saying, "Definition is 90 percent of the solution." Defining a problem is critical to guarding against merely treating the symptoms of a problem.

Excellent leaders ask five "why" questions. A reporter has five good "friends": Who, What, When, Where, How, and sometimes Why. Rather than asking "why" sometimes, managing for excellence requires that "why" *always* accompanies the basic five questions:

1. *Who* did it happen to and *why* did it happen to them?

2. *What* happened and *why* did it happen?

3. *When* did it happen and *why* did it happen then?

4. *Where* did it happen and *why* did it happen there?

5. *How* did it happen and *why* did it happen that way?

In addition to asking questions differently by always adding *why*, sharp leaders understand that their imaginations are limited by their own perceptions. Each of us has our unique KASH—our own knowledge, attitudes, skills, and habits. It clouds our imagination and perception. Excellent leaders involve others when defining material problems. Most of us will always remember the observation concerning the failure

THE LANGUAGE OF EXCELLENCE

to anticipate and prevent the events of 9/11—there was a failure of imagination.

I started my career as a CPA and transitioned to a business path after three years with Price Waterhouse. I envisioned myself as a problem solver. The difficulty was that there is always another problem right behind the current one. I wish I had understood earlier that success comes from pursuing opportunities not problems. I also discovered that most problems work themselves out. They are solved in the course of opportunity pursuits. After years of on-the-job training and observing great leaders in business, I adopted the motto below. It is an attitude about problems that will serve you well.

Not all problems deserve to be solved—of those that do, not all of them need to be solved by me.

OPPORTUNITY WEDGE

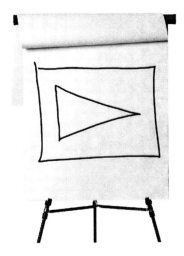

**Decisions and even the lack of
them have consequences.**

The opportunity wedge graphically illustrates that individuals and enterprises begin with a maximum range of future opportunities or alternative paths. Future opportunities narrow over time as events and decisions reduce the number of available alternative paths open to the individual or enterprise.

Change made in pursuit of opportunities eliminates other opportunities. The same can be said for the lack of purposeful change. While decisions and changes are not the same, they are closely related. Indecision and inaction have consequences on a level equal to purposeful decisions and change. The opportunity wedge conveys that each decision and indecision, each change (purposeful or not), affects future options and opportunities for a company. Business leaders who understand the opportunity wedge fight against the normal narrowing of the wedge. The company that moves from life cycle to life cycle and carefully considers the impact of their actions and inactions on the future will have an opportunity wedge that is more like an elongated open-ended box, or at a minimum, the company will have to fight to keep the right side of the wedge open.

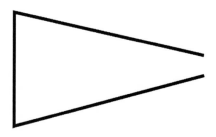

Underwood's decision that they were a typewriter company rather than a document production company narrowed the wedge to a sharp point, which led to their eventual disappearance as a company, and then as a brand. On the other hand, Steve Jobs did not limit Apple to a "computer company."

Either you as the leader make changes to keep the opportunity wedge open or natural forces close it. When it closes, the organization ceases to exist.

Excellent leaders keep their options open.

Section V

People:

The Foundation for Excellence

CAN THEY? WILL THEY?

**Who is this candidate and does he or
she have what it takes for the job?**

What makes hiring so difficult? The flip chart graphic of
a face with a question mark in the center, represents
the hiring challenge faced by organizations. The recruiter has
to uncover the answers represented by that question mark.

We humans are unique individuals so there is no such thing
as a one-for-one substitution. You do not have the option
of selecting model A or model C. The first questions to be
asked about each candidate are "Can he or she do the job?
Will he or she do the job?" If the answer to both questions is
yes, you still have to ask, "Can and will he or she do the job

in *this* environment with *our* people?" *Can* is the easy part. Whether they will or not is harder to answer. Determining whether they can and will succeed in a specific environment with specific people is difficult.

When it comes to management positions, most companies consider only one of the three choices for filling job openings. There is (1) the best mechanic, (2) the logical choice, and (3) the unknown candidate who can come from either inside or outside the organization.

Just because someone is the *best mechanic* does not mean he or she has the skills required for the management position. The best salesperson, for example, does not necessarily make the best sales manager. The typical advice is to keep your best salesperson selling. Place them in a position for which they are not qualified and everyone loses. You lose your top salesperson and gain a poor sales manager. The rest of your sales team loses under poor leadership. Eventually you will have to terminate the poor manager, or they voluntarily leave to return to what they like and do best.

The *logical choice* can also be a bad decision. Just because someone's seniority places him or her next in line, does not mean that person is the right candidate for the job.

The only right way is to select the *best fit*. That cannot happen unless you have first prepared a picture of the job. Each job has a prerequisite KASH. You have to identify the required Knowledge, Attitude, Skills, and Habits of the job in order to screen candidates. It is the KASH match between person and job that answers the question "Can they and will they?" The job pictures should also identify any traits that are best suited for success in the job environment, including coworkers and others with whom the candidate will have contact. The better the picture—the more complete and accurate it is—the better the chance that your hiring decision will be a success.

Usually the *best mechanic* and the *logical choice* selections are the symptoms of a flawed hiring approach. The important step of creating a picture of the job has been skipped. Excellent leaders will consider the *best mechanic* and the *logical choice*, as well as other alternatives. They will select, however, the candidate who best matches the job's success-oriented picture. They will look both internally and outside the organization.

While face-to-face interviews continue to be an essential part of the hiring process, the results are highly subjective and inadequate for building a top-notch team. Today, technology lets us test candidates and predict their likely success. Excellent companies take full advantage of those tools. Hiring mistakes are too costly to do otherwise.

The success-oriented company does not wait for job candidates to come to them. They proactively search for them. Ross Perot, the former presidential candidate and businessperson who founded the Electronic Data Systems, is known for the quality of the people around him. Many were ex-military, but Perot's secret to building his team of top performers rested on his hiring philosophy: "Eagles don't flock; you have to find them one at a time."

Excellent companies pull out the stops to select the best fit and act quickly to correct hiring mistakes.

THE A TEAM

To build an A team, start with A's!

The flip chart graphic is like a varsity team letter. Only the best in a particular activity or sport get to wear the letter on their jacket. Why is it important to build a varsity team, an A team? If you want to be at the top of your game as a leader, you select the best people—A-level people. Moreover, the more A's you have, the more A's will want to be on your team. Motivation is not externally created. It is prepackaged within the individual. Excellent managers and leaders learn that they cannot motivate the unmotivated.

It is a bitter lesson, but excellent leaders learn that they cannot change the individual but they can change people.

Excellent managers do just that. They understand that hiring or *keeping* the wrong person extinguishes motivation in others. A-level people demand A-level performance from their peers. When you allow less, you weaken the entire team.

The best leaders sell a vision of how individuals can achieve their goals by achieving the organization's goals. Motivated people want to belong to something that recognizes their individual value. If you want the right people on the bus, you start with the right people. Outstanding organizations look for people who want to travel north—on I-65 North. Sunday drivers need not apply. People who want to travel south, east, or west should look elsewhere.

Steve Jobs put it this way: A-level people want to be part of an organization of A-level people.

RIGHT PEOPLE ON THE BUS

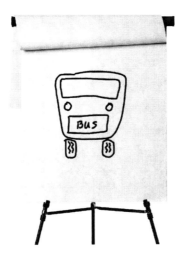

**The wheels go round and round, but
it is what's inside that counts!**

The flip chart graphic of a bus is taken from a reference by Jim Collins in his book *Good to Great*. He used the bus to represent the leadership team of an enterprise. They are the people leading an organization on its journey. What does it take for an enterprise to go from good to great? Jim Collins called it "getting the right people on the bus." He spent years researching the difference between most enterprises and those who, in his judgment, made the transition from good to great. His conclusion would not have been a surprise to Steve Jobs, who changed the world as the leader of Apple. *The key is having the right people.*

As mentioned in the previous section, Jobs believed that A-level people want to work with A-level people. In the typical organization, A-level people leave to go in search of A-level job opportunities. The B- and C-level people left behind begin to become the status quo over time. That is why, in a turnaround situation, "getting the wrong people off the bus" to make room for A-level replacements becomes the first job of management.

How do you get the right people? It is not easy. Involve your A-level people in the selection process. Use an employment testing service. Hire successful people. Nevertheless, be prepared to get mistakes off the bus fast. It takes time to assemble an A-team. It is like making fine brandy; your team has to be distilled over time. Hire carefully and refine by removing and replacing those who do not fit.

You are only a leader—it takes having the right people following you to go from good to great.

AUTHORITY TRIANGLE

**Fully competent employees don't
show up for work on day one.**

This flip chart image illustrates that the decision-making ability of newcomers (the overlaid light gray authority triangle) is the reverse of fully competent employees' ability, the original darker triangle. Individuals on the job can make three kinds of decisions:

1. Do it

2. Do it and then report it

3. Recommend and ask before acting

When sales goals are not being achieved, when customers are complaining about the availability of support, when production is falling behind demand, the standard answer is always the same—add personnel. The new resources are brought online, sales decline, customer service worsens, and production falls further behind. What is going on?

It is the downward spike of the change curve, and it can be explained by the authority triangle. The fully competent incumbent makes the first type of decision, the *just do it* ones, about 80 percent of the time. They make the second type of decision somewhere around 15 percent of the time. Those are the decisions that can be reversed or modified when reported. Only 5 percent of the time do they delay action until authorized to act.

For new employees, the authority triangle is reversed so that most of the time new employees ask permission before acting. That consumes productive resources and thus reduces the total output of the unit. For successful additions, the authority triangle rotates properly over time so that they begin to increase productivity rather than lower it.

Unfortunately, not every promoted worker or every new hire can and will do the job in the environment with the people involved. Those who turn their triangle too slowly (Sunday drivers) continue to be a drain on productivity. Those whose rotation of the triangle is too fast (reckless drivers) create an undue risk to the organization by acting before they have the competence required.

When the rotation is too slow or too fast, an effective leader must take corrective action, or they will subject the organization to unnecessary damage.

The authority triangle is an important concept in evaluating new additions and promotions—guard against reckless as well as Sunday drivers.

MACK TRUCK RULE

No one is indispensable.

Mack trucks, like the one represented by the flip chart drawing, are big eighteen-wheelers. Any member of the team could be run over by one on the way home from work. That absurd image appropriately illustrates the equally absurd fallacy that any member of the team is indispensable. They cannot be indispensable because, by nature or by accident, *we are all dispensable.*

Every business or organization leader at one time or another will have to deal with the argument that a significant salary increase or promotion is required because the recipient is indispensable. No matter how much someone's salary is increased or other rewards are granted, tomorrow morning that person's position could be vacant by the individual's choice or by uncontrollable events—such as the Mack truck.

Excessive compensation or special accommodations are the wrong way to deal with the "indispensable" person. The only solution to a seemingly indispensable person is to make him or her dispensable. Anything else places the organization at risk. Solve the problem by focusing on adding capacity and capability through hiring or training others.

For the excellent leader, the indispensable person is an undue risk to be avoided through training or adding capacity.

MAJORING IN MINORS

One thing is for sure—they *look* busy!

T he overloaded in- and out-box graphic represents the individual who majors in minors. They fill up everyone's in- and out-box (snail or e-mail) with reports, memos, requests, proposals, projects, etc., etc., etc. Activity, hard work, and long hours are not synonymous with contribution. Contribution results from concentrating on the *main* things success depends on and consuming the *minimum* resources required to achieve the objective.

Parkinson's Law discussed earlier is the observation that "work expands to fill available time" and, by extension, "expenses rise to meet income." It is the idea that work creates work. Excellent leaders must be constantly diligent and alert—always simplifying and eliminating. As previously noted, that is the ability governments and bureaucracies seem unable to master, but effective business leaders must. Without leading the organization in a continuing effort to simplify and eliminate the unnecessary, negative forces will drive the business into unsustainable levels of inefficiency.

People who major in minors misdirect efforts away from the main goals and, as predicted by Parkinson's Law, they create work for others—work that too often is not essential for success. Excellent leaders understand the difference between contribution and activity and accept their obligation to purge those majoring in minors from the organization.

**People who major in minors may look busy,
but it is at the expense of everyone else.**

BUSINESSMAN CONCEPT

Act and make decisions as if it were your business.

One of the things any effective leader would like to instill in each of his or her team members is the feeling that it is "my business." You are the businessperson. It is your reputation. Your money is on the line.

As a college student, I worked at night at the Tastee Bread Company in Nashville, Tennessee. Their motto was "Baked while you sleep." The company had a suggestion box and rewarded employees monetarily for suggestions that saved money or improved productivity. A member of the maintenance department measured the water being lost by a leaky faucet and applied the utility's rate to calculate the cost of water being lost yearly. He entered a suggestion that the bad washer causing the leak be replaced. The suggestion even included his calculation of the dollar amount the replaced washer would save the company. The next day, after the suggestion box had been opened and his suggestion read, he was fired.

You see, he was the *maintenance* man. It was his job to repair the faucet. Something he would have done if he had looked at the Tastee Bread Company as *his* business. With a common sense of direction and an understanding of the rules of the road, you will make the right decisions and avoid the wrong ones as long as you treat the organization as your own business.

It is *your* business—just stay on I-65 North!

TERMINATIONS

There are plenty of rules, but no right way.

The flip chart for terminations is blank for a very good reason. In spite of what the human resources people will tell you, there is no right way to terminate people. Yes, there is the three-step method:

1. Agree there is a problem

2. Agree on what is required to correct it and by what specific date

3. Agree on the consequence(s) if the corrective action does not occur

I have not pulled punches when it comes to letting people go. You cannot be an excellent leader unless you are prepared to get the wrong people off the bus. However, it is never easy.

There are people you want to march to the door immediately, and they deserve it. There are people who just cannot get along. There are those who will not follow the playbook. There are people who continue to insist that the organization should go south, east, or west rather than north. There are people in over their head—they do not have the KASH needed for the job. Then there are those who seem to do everything needed to succeed but, for whatever reason, just cannot achieve the objectives. You have an obligation to put someone new in their position who you believe can take the company where it needs to go.

When you cut through all the reasons, it comes down to two groups of people. Those who deserve to be terminated because of their performance and those who are hiring or promotion mistakes.

Everyone makes mistakes, but if you are in a leadership position, then either you are up to the job of correcting those mistakes—or you are the one who needs to be on the street looking for a job. As hard as it may be at times, it is your job to build a winning team and that means cutting people as well as giving new people a chance to play on the team. If it is your mistake, you need to go the extra mile to help the individual move on to a position inside or outside the company where you believe they can be successful. That means giving them the time to relocate or at least providing them with a generous separation arrangement.

We live in a very litigious time, and our government is continuously coming up with laws and regulations designed to
protect employees. The hiring and firing functions are mine-
fields that should be navigated with great care.

When it comes to hiring, it is your job to determine if
a candidate fits the job picture: *Can and will he or she do
the job in this environment with these people?* There are all
kinds of interview questions that are off the table because of
government rules. That makes your job of hiring the right
people more difficult, but that does not relieve you of your
responsibility. You have to know the rules, and you have to
acquire the skills to get the job done within those rules.

When it comes to terminations, it is one thing to terminate
someone immediately for misconduct; it is altogether different
when there is no misconduct. Fairness requires that you deal
with each case in light of the circumstances. Yet at the same
time, treating people differently exposes you and the company
to the risk of litigation. That is why many companies have
rules providing for notice or separation pay based on length
of employment. Nevertheless, before there is an issue of termination, there is nothing to prevent you from counseling an
individual about where their talents lie and what their future
prospects are within your organization. There is nothing to
stop you from helping someone secure a position elsewhere.
*The best resolution of a hiring or promotion mistake is one that
does not result in termination.* Having just said that, there is
such a thing as "constructive" termination. There is a blurry
line between counseling and constructively firing someone. It
is a line for you to find and respect.

I started my career as a CPA with a national firm. Very few hires in a national CPA firm become partners. Most leave as I did to join a client of the firm. The CPA firm had an active alumni program with newsletters and periodic alumni events. The firm had developed a method of orderly migration to make room for incoming candidates—potential future partners. For those who left at the encouragement of the CPA firm, being an alumnus was a status symbol rather than a "termination" on their résumé.

The idea of "in this environment with these people," means that just because a person did not work out in a particular situation does not mean they will not be a success elsewhere. That is an important message. It is particularly important in those situations where a hiring or promotion mistake has occurred. The concept is helpful when counseling an individual about his or her future. It helps when recommending someone to other employers. If counseling does not solve the problem, the concept is helpful when you terminate a person. You can do so without branding that person as a failure. Your action is only communicating that the individual did not work out in this environment with these people, but does not necessarily mean that the individual will not succeed elsewhere—in a different environment with different people.

Excellent leaders have a responsibility for mistakes made during the hiring process but no obligation to people who earned termination.

Section VI

ACTION:

THE FINAL INGREDIENT FOR EXCELLENCE

TNT: TODAY NOT TOMORROW

Nothing happens until something happens.

The flip chart graphic, a lighted stick of dynamite, emphasizes the "big bang" role of the leader. Leaders make things happen. They make them happen now—*today*, not tomorrow!

Excellent leaders create momentum, a sense of urgency and enthusiasm, by encouraging an environment of acting today not tomorrow (TNT). Even large opportunities, problems, and issues can be broken down into smaller steps (actions) that can be acted upon incrementally to deal with issues in a TNT manner. Today-not-tomorrow is a simplifying tactic.

In my last company, I placed a sign in both the accounting and shipping areas that read: *Bill it today. Ship it today.* Without that performance standard, we would have required systems in place to keep up with what had not been billed and what had not been shipped. TNT reduced our workload.

In addition to creating forward momentum, enthusiasm, and reducing work, TNT is the right method for managing new projects and developing activities—small, fast, and simple. Break the effort into quick-turnaround projects—build a model, test it with clients. *Act–test–act!*

TNT—"Do it today, not tomorrow"—is the mantra of the excellent leader.

Section VII

EXECUTIVE OVERVIEW

Section I

I-65 North: The Pursuit of Excellence

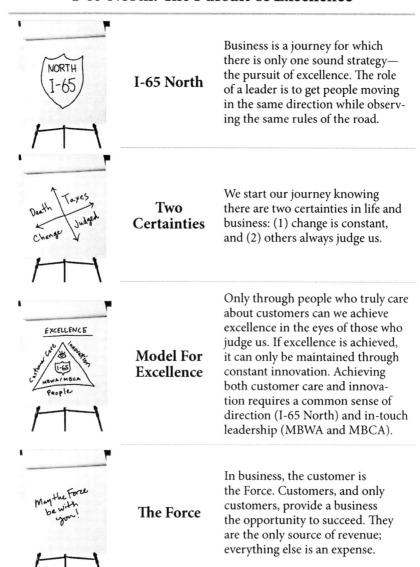

NORTH I-65	**I-65 North**	Business is a journey for which there is only one sound strategy—the pursuit of excellence. The role of a leader is to get people moving in the same direction while observing the same rules of the road.
Death Taxes Change Judged	**Two Certainties**	We start our journey knowing there are two certainties in life and business: (1) change is constant, and (2) others always judge us.
EXCELLENCE Customer Care Innovation I-65 MBWA/MBCA People	**Model For Excellence**	Only through people who truly care about customers can we achieve excellence in the eyes of those who judge us. If excellence is achieved, it can only be maintained through constant innovation. Achieving both customer care and innovation requires a common sense of direction (I-65 North) and in-touch leadership (MBWA and MBCA).
May the Force be with you!	**The Force**	In business, the customer is the Force. Customers, and only customers, provide a business the opportunity to succeed. They are the only source of revenue; everything else is an expense.

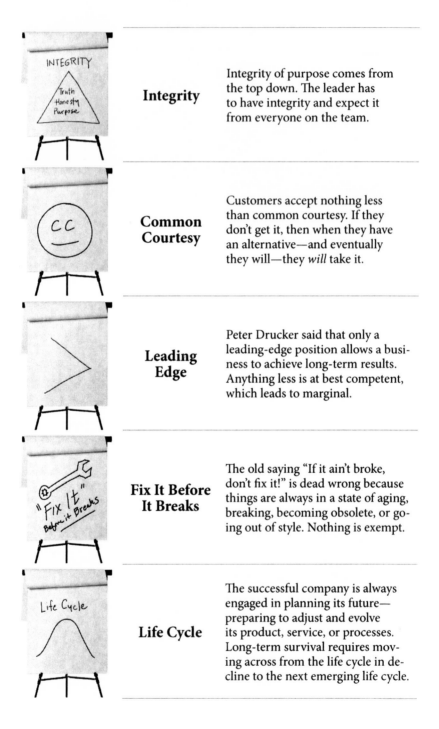

Integrity

Integrity of purpose comes from the top down. The leader has to have integrity and expect it from everyone on the team.

Common Courtesy

Customers accept nothing less than common courtesy. If they don't get it, then when they have an alternative—and eventually they will—they *will* take it.

Leading Edge

Peter Drucker said that only a leading-edge position allows a business to achieve long-term results. Anything less is at best competent, which leads to marginal.

Fix It Before It Breaks

The old saying "If it ain't broke, don't fix it!" is dead wrong because things are always in a state of aging, breaking, becoming obsolete, or going out of style. Nothing is exempt.

Life Cycle

The successful company is always engaged in planning its future—preparing to adjust and evolve its product, service, or processes. Long-term survival requires moving across from the life cycle in decline to the next emerging life cycle.

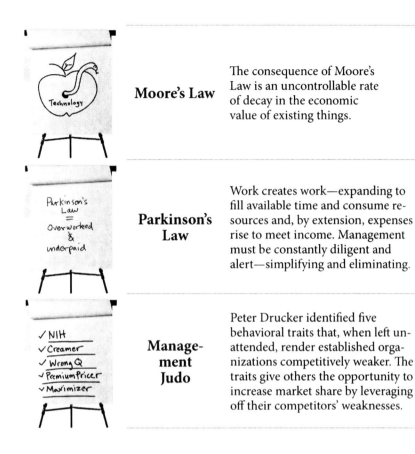

	Moore's Law	The consequence of Moore's Law is an uncontrollable rate of decay in the economic value of existing things.
	Parkinson's Law	Work creates work—expanding to fill available time and consume resources and, by extension, expenses rise to meet income. Management must be constantly diligent and alert—simplifying and eliminating.
	Management Judo	Peter Drucker identified five behavioral traits that, when left unattended, render established organizations competitively weaker. The traits give others the opportunity to increase market share by leveraging off their competitors' weaknesses.

Section II

Change: The Path to Excellence

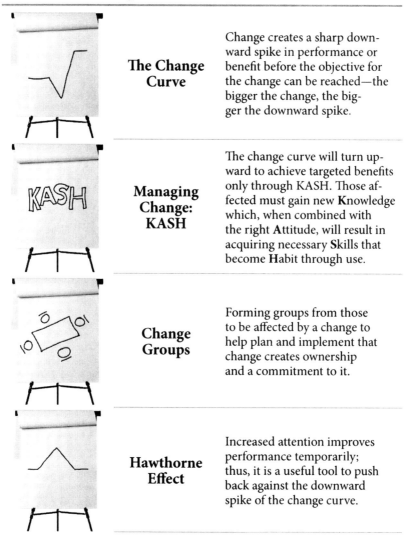

	The Change Curve	Change creates a sharp downward spike in performance or benefit before the objective for the change can be reached—the bigger the change, the bigger the downward spike.
	Managing Change: KASH	The change curve will turn upward to achieve targeted benefits only through KASH. Those affected must gain new Knowledge which, when combined with the right Attitude, will result in acquiring necessary Skills that become Habit through use.
	Change Groups	Forming groups from those to be affected by a change to help plan and implement that change creates ownership and a commitment to it.
	Hawthorne Effect	Increased attention improves performance temporarily; thus, it is a useful tool to push back against the downward spike of the change curve.

	Ceremo-nialism	Nothing encourages success more than success itself; there-fore, awards and recognition tied to KASH create an upward push against the downward spike caused by change.
	Limited Resources	Resources have to be deployed to become productive, but deploy-ing them consumes existing resources and energy. Like the neck of an hourglass, deploy-ment limits access to resources.
	Relative Perception	The downward spike of the change curve is relative to the size, or even the perception of the size, of the change.
	Incremen-talism	Rather than one big change, a series of smaller changes is likely to get you where you want to be, faster and at a lower cost and risk. The right way to implement change is proportional to the ability of the organization to deal with and absorb the downward spike of the change curve.
	Change by Decree	One of the wrong ways to initiate change is by decree: "Do it because I said to!" or "Do it because I'm the boss." This is unmanaged; thus, it could arbitrarily succeed or fail.

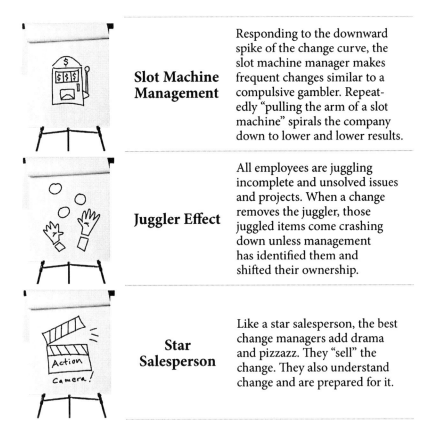

	Slot Machine Management	Responding to the downward spike of the change curve, the slot machine manager makes frequent changes similar to a compulsive gambler. Repeatedly "pulling the arm of a slot machine" spirals the company down to lower and lower results.
	Juggler Effect	All employees are juggling incomplete and unsolved issues and projects. When a change removes the juggler, those juggled items come crashing down unless management has identified them and shifted their ownership.
	Star Salesperson	Like a star salesperson, the best change managers add drama and pizzazz. They "sell" the change. They also understand change and are prepared for it.

Section III

Management: Guidelines for Excellence

Management Cycle

Modern day jobs require management skills. Management is planning, organizing, acting, and controlling—a continuous cycle of processing input, taking action, collecting feedback, and repeating the process.

Five Things

Successful organizations do five things:
- Engage in planning
- Set goals and objectives
- Develop plans
- Prepare for opportunities & contingencies
- Measure and hold people accountable

Temporary Targets

Plans are based on assumptions about the future; thus, planning is doomed to fail unless the plan includes changing the plan as the future becomes clearer. Objectives are only temporary targets.

Count the Teeth

Planning is not an intellectual forum for speculating on that which is determinable.

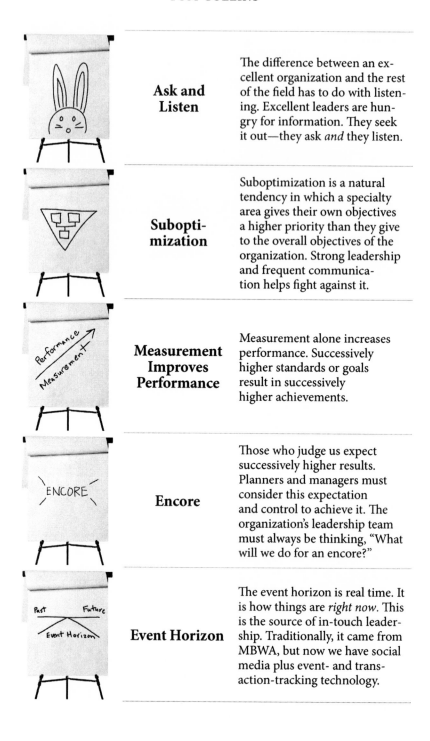

Ask and Listen

The difference between an excellent organization and the rest of the field has to do with listening. Excellent leaders are hungry for information. They seek it out—they ask *and* they listen.

Suboptimization

Suboptimization is a natural tendency in which a specialty area gives their own objectives a higher priority than they give to the overall objectives of the organization. Strong leadership and frequent communication helps fight against it.

Measurement Improves Performance

Measurement alone increases performance. Successively higher standards or goals result in successively higher achievements.

Encore

Those who judge us expect successively higher results. Planners and managers must consider this expectation and control to achieve it. The organization's leadership team must always be thinking, "What will we do for an encore?"

Event Horizon

The event horizon is real time. It is how things are *right now*. This is the source of in-touch leadership. Traditionally, it came from MBWA, but now we have social media plus event- and transaction-tracking technology.

	Management Candy	There are right ways and wrong ways to pursue objectives. Management candy, or M&M's, represents the right way: Do the *Main* things necessary to achieve the objective with the *Minimum* resources required. It is about doing the right things the right way.
	Rule of the Fewest	The fewer things you have to deal with, the easier it is to achieve a given result. Conversely, the more things you have to deal with, the more resources you need to achieve a given result.
	Sunk Cost	Cost previously incurred is not important to the decision-making process. For example, the original cost of a ship under water is not relevant. Only the costs of raising and reconditioning it versus the cost of a new ship are relevant.
	Playbook	The playbook icon illustrates that planning is about communication and coordination. The objective is to empower members of the team by giving a clear sense of direction and the rules of the road for getting there.

Section IV

Opportunities: Strategies for Excellence

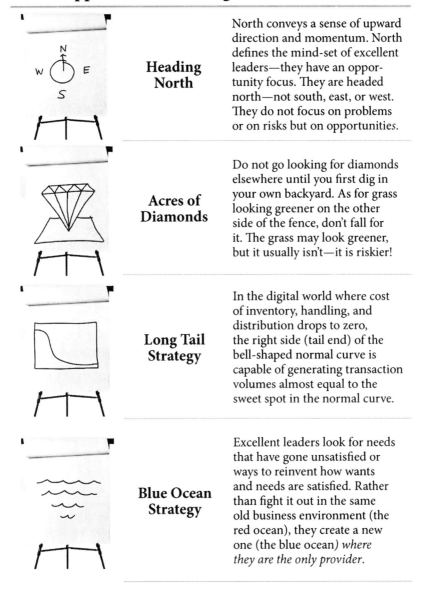

	Heading North	North conveys a sense of upward direction and momentum. North defines the mind-set of excellent leaders—they have an opportunity focus. They are headed north—not south, east, or west. They do not focus on problems or on risks but on opportunities.
	Acres of Diamonds	Do not go looking for diamonds elsewhere until you first dig in your own backyard. As for grass looking greener on the other side of the fence, don't fall for it. The grass may look greener, but it usually isn't—it is riskier!
	Long Tail Strategy	In the digital world where cost of inventory, handling, and distribution drops to zero, the right side (tail end) of the bell-shaped normal curve is capable of generating transaction volumes almost equal to the sweet spot in the normal curve.
	Blue Ocean Strategy	Excellent leaders look for needs that have gone unsatisfied or ways to reinvent how wants and needs are satisfied. Rather than fight it out in the same old business environment (the red ocean), they create a new one (the blue ocean) *where they are the only provider.*

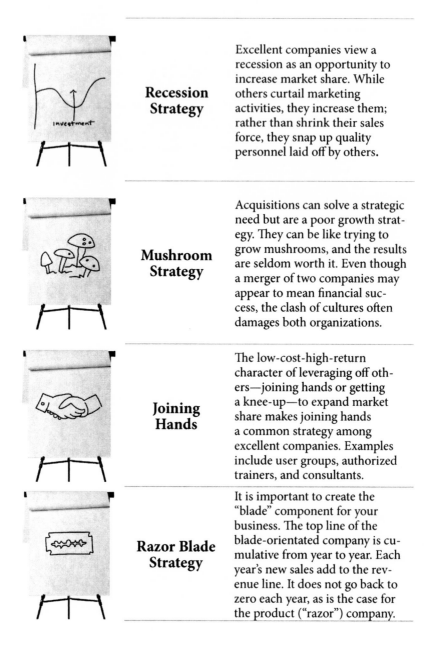

Recession Strategy

Excellent companies view a recession as an opportunity to increase market share. While others curtail marketing activities, they increase them; rather than shrink their sales force, they snap up quality personnel laid off by others.

Mushroom Strategy

Acquisitions can solve a strategic need but are a poor growth strategy. They can be like trying to grow mushrooms, and the results are seldom worth it. Even though a merger of two companies may appear to mean financial success, the clash of cultures often damages both organizations.

Joining Hands

The low-cost-high-return character of leveraging off others—joining hands or getting a knee-up—to expand market share makes joining hands a common strategy among excellent companies. Examples include user groups, authorized trainers, and consultants.

Razor Blade Strategy

It is important to create the "blade" component for your business. The top line of the blade-orientated company is cumulative from year to year. Each year's new sales add to the revenue line. It does not go back to zero each year, as is the case for the product ("razor") company.

	Luck Favors the Prepared	Change is the stuff of opportunities—provided you have developed a way of thinking that prepares the firm to take advantage of whatever the future brings. French scientist Louis Pasteur said, "Chance favors only the prepared mind." Practicing "what ifs" as a team can prepare you for surprise opportunities.
	Completion Rule	The last percentage of any project carries the greatest risk and cost. The rule for project completion is that it is complete (ready for initial release) when 80 percent of the ultimate design is 100 percent finished. Leave something for the encore.
	Circle of Secrecy	While management cannot keep a secret, with the knowledge of your team you can manage the rate of expansion in the circle of those who know it. Code names are one of the tools for doing so.
	Problem Policy	Not all problems deserve to be solved; of those that do, not all of them need to be solved by you. When you do tackle a problem, you should have a no-return policy. Define the root cause. Don't treat symptoms; solve the problem so it will not come up again.
	Opportunity Wedge	The opportunity wedge conveys that each decision and indecision, each change (purposeful or not) impacts future options and opportunities for a company—the normal narrowing of the wedge.

Section V

People: The Foundation for Excellence

Can they?
Will they?

When hiring, the questions that have to be asked about each individual are: Can he or she do the job? Will he or she do the job? In this environment with our people?

The A Team

People want to belong to something that recognizes their individual value. If you want the right people on the bus, you start with the right people. Steve Jobs put it this way: "A-level people want to be part of an organization of A-level people."

Right People on the Bus

Jim Collins noted that in a turnaround situation, "getting the wrong people off the bus" to make room for A-level replacements becomes the first job of management.

Authority Triangle

Until the authority triangle is turned, new additions consume rather than contribute productive capacity. Those flipping the triangle too fast put the organization at risk. Too slow, and they continue to be a burden rather than an asset.

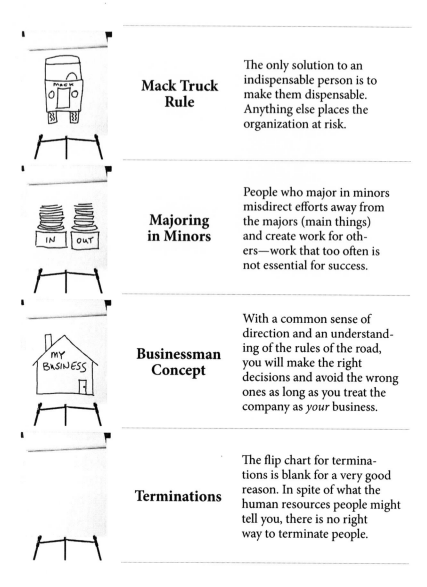

	Mack Truck Rule	The only solution to an indispensable person is to make them dispensable. Anything else places the organization at risk.
	Majoring in Minors	People who major in minors misdirect efforts away from the majors (main things) and create work for others—work that too often is not essential for success.
	Businessman Concept	With a common sense of direction and an understanding of the rules of the road, you will make the right decisions and avoid the wrong ones as long as you treat the company as *your* business.
	Terminations	The flip chart for terminations is blank for a very good reason. In spite of what the human resources people might tell you, there is no right way to terminate people.

Section VI

Action: The Final Ingredient for Excellence

TNT: Today Not Tomorrow

Excellent leaders create a sense of urgency and strive to create an environment of acting today not tomorrow. TNT is a simplifying tactic.

ABOUT TOM COLLINS

Author, Entrepreneur, and Epicurean

The London-based publication *Citytech* called him an "out-standing individual and visionary" when M. Thomas (Tom) Collins was named as one of the Top 100 Global Tech Leaders in the legal community. Tom is also the recipient of the Lifetime Achievement Award from the US publication *Law Technology News* for his contribution to the use of technology in the legal community. Although now retired from the commercial world, he continues to write and speak on management and pen his Mark Rollins adventure series of mysteries.

www.I65North.com

Tom Collins is available for selected readings and lectures. To inquire about a possible appearance, contact PLA Media at 615-327-0100 or info@plamedia.com. To contact him directly, e-mail tom.collins@markrollinsadventures.com.

CPSIA information can be obtained at www.ICGtesting.com
Printed in the USA
LVOW07*1933260216

476877LV00002B/7/P